"How to" guide

Looking after your Donors

Karen Gilchrist

DIRECTORY OF SOCIAL CHANGE

CAF

Published by
The Directory of Social Change
24 Stephenson Way
London NW1 2DP
Tel: 020 7209 5151, fax: 020 7209 5049
e-mail: info@dsc.org.uk
from whom further copies and a full publications list are available

The Directory of Social Change is a Registered Charity no. 800517

ISBN 1 900360 76 4

British Library Cataloguing in Publication Data
A catalogue record for this book is available from the British Library

Cover design by Lenn Darroux
Designed by Sarah Nicholson
Typeset, printed and bound by Stephen Austin, Hertford

Other Directory of Social Change departments in London:
Courses and Conferences tel: 020 7209 4949
Charity Centre tel: 020 7209 1015
Research tel: 020 7209 4422
Finance and Administration tel: 020 7209 0902

Directory of Social Change Northern Office:
Federation House, Hope Street, Liverpool L1 9BW
Courses and Conferences tel: 0151 708 0117
Research tel: 0151 708 0136

Contents

About the author

Karen Gilchrist is a researcher and writer. She is the director of the media and communications company Resource Base, which works in social, educational and cultural affairs. She has been a cross-media coordinator with the charity Community Service Volunteers and worked for TVS Education and Community before helping to set up Resource Base.

Introduction

There's always a thrill when you open an envelope and a cheque drops out, or when you receive a phone call offering your group a donation. You have finally managed to persuade someone to part with their money in support of your good cause.

Sometimes this can seem like an end in itself – after all the hard work you have put in. Actually it's the beginning: of a new relationship with a donor who might give to your organisation again.

If you look after your donors then the chances are that you will raise more money from them in the future. This is true whether the donor is an organisation or an individual. We are going to look at both types of supporter in this book.

We want to help you think about who your donors are and what they need; how you can show your appreciation for their support; and how you might sensitively approach them for additional donations in the future.

In smaller charities and community groups one or two people will do most of the fundraising and be responsible for looking after all donors. Larger charities might have different people or departments focusing on individual donors (or members), trusts and foundations, corporate donors, and public funders. We look at all of these groups of donors in this book, and there are hints to help you whether you are a single fundraiser or member of a specialist fundraising department.

The importance of building a relationship

This book is not just about asking the same people for support two or three times. It is about developing different relationships with the people and organisations who have made a donation. And it's important to remember that a relationship is a two-way process. You need to listen to their views, try to understand what they want, and work with them rather than simply sending out the odd newsletter followed by a request for more money.

They might want to look after you too!

Another thing to remember is that some of your donors – particularly the larger trusts or companies – will want to look after you too. Many are keen to develop relationships or partnerships with the groups they fund. This might affect how you approach them, and so you need to tailor everything you do to reflect their individual approach.

Your unique mix of donors

This guide gives general tips and advice. You will need to think carefully about how to apply it in your particular case. Every group has its own unique mix of donors. You might even know them all by name. If you have regular contact with them, then, rather than mailing out information, you might want to hand over any leaflets in person.

What is in this guide?

We begin, in Chapter 1, with a look at some of the reasons why you should look after your donors. It's mostly common sense. But there might be some things that you haven't considered. It will certainly help you to explain the importance of this work to your trustees and colleagues.

Once you are convinced that it's a good idea to look after your donors you need to put together a plan of action. This will help you to limit the time you spend on this area, as well as giving you an idea of the costs involved. Planning is the focus of Chapter 2.

We have already said that every organisation has its own unique mix of donors. In Chapter 3 we describe how you might analyse your existing supporters.

Once you know just who supports you (and perhaps why) you can start to research other potential donors. We touch on this in Chapter 4.

Then we look at how you might secure repeat donations from both organisations and individuals. We give an overview in Chapter 5.

The rest of the guide is divided into two – first we look at organisations, then individuals.

In Chapter 6 we explore some of the ways you can benefit again from organisations.

Chapters 7 and 8 look at some of the techniques you can use to develop your relationships with organisations – through keeping them informed, showing them your work, involving them in decisions, and giving them due credit for their support.

In Chapter 9 we turn our attention to individuals, and some of the ways you can benefit again from them. Chapters 10 and 11 focus on ways of building your relationships with individuals – by staying in touch, involving them in your work and decisions, and thanking them sufficiently.

Evaluation is very important in all areas of fundraising. It can make a significant difference to your approach to repeat donations and donor relationships. We run through some of the issues and options in Chapter 12.

Finally, in *Further information*, we signpost some useful organisations and resources providing further information and advice.

1

Why look after your donors?

There are many reasons why you should look after your donors, and we explore some of these in this chapter. For one thing it's good manners – if someone has given you support then you should really show your appreciation.

In this chapter we cover:

- The reasons why it is important to look after your donors
- The benefits to your organisation of repeat donations
- The opportunity to learn from your existing donors

Courtesy

When you give something to someone – whether it's money, advice or a meal – you expect to hear from them afterwards. The same is true for your donors; they can reasonably expect you to keep in touch. It's not just about saying 'thank you', though this is very important. It's also about demonstrating your gratitude.

Reassurance

People give their money in good faith. They expect a cheque to arrive in the post. They believe the street collection will reach its intended destination. And they trust you to use the money as you have promised. Even though charities have a legal obligation to use donated money for a stated purpose, it is always good practice to reassure your donors.

If you stay in touch and show them your work in progress, they will be reassured. Your donors will know that they have spent their money wisely. If they give another donation, then it will be in safe hands. Public confidence is important. A study by Henley Management College found that people who don't give to charity think only 45% of donations is spent on the actual cause. Regular donors think the figure is 67%, but in reality, an average 80% of a donation goes directly to the cause.

Repeat donations

If you look after your donors, they will remember you; feel good about you; and be receptive to your appeals for additional money. Instead of 'cold calling' or 'cold mailing' you will be 'warm calling' and 'warm mailing'.

There are various stages you need people to move through when you want a response to an appeal for funds. In simplified marketing terms they move through the four stages: Attention, Interest, Desire and Action (AIDA).

When you approach your well-cared-for donors, it will be easier to get their Attention (they know all about you). They have already shown general Interest in your work. As you get to know them better you will learn more about their cares and concerns, and what might capture their imagination.

Similarly you will have a good understanding of what motivates your donors. You will then be able to encourage them to Desire to help you. And they will be likely to take Action. After all, they've done so before (and regarded it as a wise move). What you need to ensure, though, is that you make it easy for them to respond.

It is important to remember the call to action. All too often charities get quite close to many of their donors – keeping them informed and involved – and then they forget to ask for extra support. Some feel embarrassed, some assume their donors will understand the need for funds, and others don't realise that their existing donors are the ones most likely to give to their appeal.

Occasionally people will give without being prompted. Most of us need a more direct approach. We need to be asked in clear and simple terms. And we want help to respond. That might be a reply-paid envelope, someone to help us fill out a form for Give-As-You-Earn, the right words to include in our will...

The financial benefits are tremendous. It is estimated to cost five times more to recruit a new donor than to secure more funding from an existing supporter. In an article entitled 'Improving donor retention: how can charities build loyalty?' in *Dimensions 2000, Volume 2* (see *Further information*), Adrian Sargeant explains how donors are 'lost' or become inactive over time. The graph opposite, reproduced from that article, shows the rate of donor attrition over a five-year period.

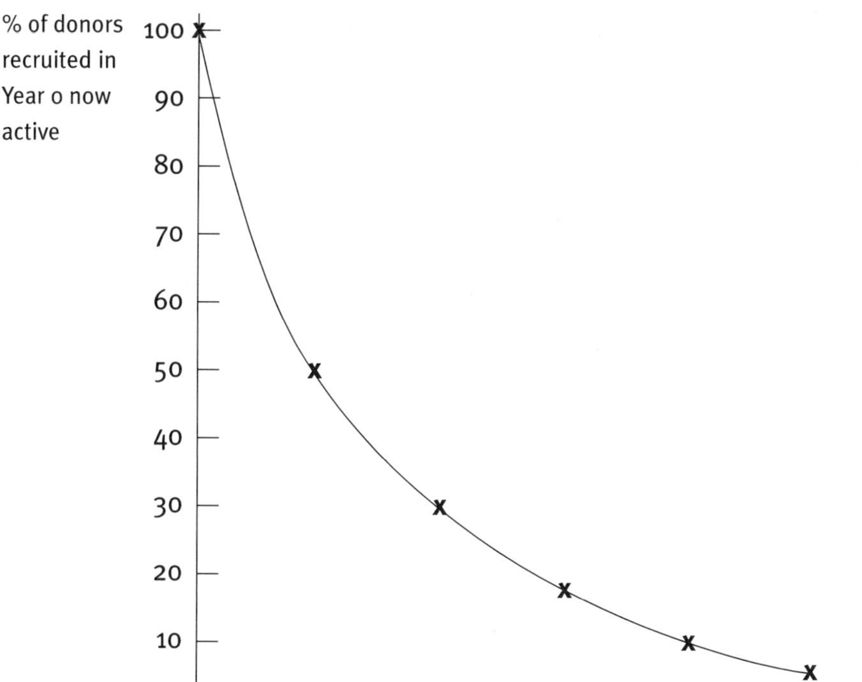

Better targeting

As you look after your donors you will get to know more about them. You can build up information on a database – about their levels of commitment, what interests them, their personal circumstances and so on. As you understand them better you can become more sophisticated in how you approach them.

You can target certain individuals and organisations with a request that's bound to interest them. You can talk to others at different times about an appeal that's more likely to engage them.

Your donors will feel you know them well, and will appreciate not receiving irrelevant requests. And your organisation stands to benefit when you spend less on well-targeted appeals in relation to the amounts raised.

Keeping up with developments

Your donors will probably include organisations such as trusts, companies and public bodies. Developing your relationships with these supporters will enable you to know when and how circumstances change. For example you may hear when people are moving jobs – either within their organisation or between organisations. You will be able to keep in touch and continue your personal relationship with them, whilst getting to know new people.

You will get to know about an organisation's changing priorities or funding policies. And you might hear about new funding opportunities from different parts of the organisation.

At the same time your existing funders probably meet other funders through professional networks (such as the Association of Charitable Foundations and the Corporate Responsibility Group). So you might hear about new funding developments through your existing donor. You might even be recommended to other funders through such a network.

In the *Dimensions 2000* report into patterns of funding by grant-making trusts (*Dimensions 2000, Volume 3: Patterns of independent grantmaking in the UK*, see *Further information*) it was found that 'trusts often consult each other both formally and informally about groups and projects that have applied to them'.

A small educational charity received research funding from a major foundation. The project was to explore alternative educational opportunities for disadvantaged young people, particularly those excluded from school.

The foundation attended regular advisory group meetings as the project progressed. At one of these meetings the group discussed a creative research programme involving young people with mental health problems. A week later another trust contacted the educational charity, inviting it to apply under its 'young people at risk' scheme.

This came about following a lunch reception attended by a representative from the major foundation funding the charity. He chatted to a trustee from the other trust and explained the outline proposal. The trustee felt the project had potential and fitted his trust's criteria, so he approached the educational charity running the research programme.

By staying in regular contact with all donors you are also likely to hear when people change their addresses and contact details. This will enable you to keep track of your past donors. Your database will be fairly up-to-date.

Cross-fertilisation of ideas

Most community groups calculate the amount of money they need to raise for a particular project. They then approach individuals and organisations to ask for support. However, if you have an ongoing relationship with your funders, they might develop an idea or project in partnership with you. If they help to develop the idea then they are likely to support it or help find support from other funders they know.

Even if this doesn't happen, you may hear about new ideas and developments in the voluntary sector through your organisational funders.

You could hear about someone else's exciting project, funded by one of your supporters, which inspires you to do something similar for your own organisation. This is all about sharing good practice.

Finding a pattern and identifying new donors

Another extremely important reason for looking after your current donors is that it helps you to spot new ones. Once you understand why people and organisations give to you, you can identify other similar individuals and bodies, and target them in the future. Your existing donors might even help with this, by distributing your literature and recommending you to friends and colleagues. Their personal testimonies can be more effective because they are seen as independent from the charity's own staff.

2

Planning

As you start to think about your donors and how best to look after them, you may well come up with a hundred and one good ideas about how to stay in touch and make them feel good about you. These ideas need to be manageable, otherwise you could spend all your time (and resources) on your donors and none on your good cause. Conversely, if you don't have a 'donor development plan' this area of your work might be neglected or under-resourced. Planning is important, and that's the focus of this chapter.

You will find out in this chapter:

- The importance of producing a donor development plan
- What to include in this development plan
- How to produce targets and budgets for donor development

The need for a plan

It is good practice to prepare written plans for different areas of work – so that you can work effectively and so that your trustees/management committee are aware of, and support, what you are doing. It also means if you move into a different role within the organisation, or are away for any reason, it is easy for one of your colleagues to continue the work.

A plan for donor development, or donor relations, can help you to:

- identify (some of) the time involved;
- set a general budget for this activity (as distinct from individual fundraising appeals);
- work out whether or not you have sufficient computer resources for what you have planned (to store and analyse the information you gather);
- use everybody's contacts effectively (avoiding duplication);
- ensure that your promotional materials give clear and consistent messages;
- keep your communications regular and well spaced across the year;
- ensure you are clear about everyone's roles and responsibilities.

Building a plan

What, then, might be in such a plan?

Aims and objectives

It's always a good idea to begin any plan with a statement of why you are doing something, and what you hope to achieve. This will ensure that everyone involved is in agreement about the purpose of this work. And it will also help you to evaluate your work.

First you should sum up why you are looking after your donors – what you hope to achieve. This is your overall aim. Your aim might be to increase the loyalty and commitment of your donors, through regular communication and appropriate involvement – or something along these lines.

You can get more specific when it comes to the objectives. These outline individual, achievable steps to help you meet your overall aim. You might wish to:

- increase the number of repeat donations;
- increase the size of repeat donations;
- increase the number of donors giving in a more regular and committed way;
- involve donors more often in decision making;
- involve donors more often in the group's activities;
- understand the profile of donors better;
- find new donors, using data on existing donors as a guide.

Such objectives can help to give your work a clear structure. They will also enable you to set goals, or targets.

Setting targets

Goals or targets translate your objectives into figures. Your targets should be realistic, achievable and measurable.

You might work through each of your objectives, setting specific targets for one, two or three years.

The first objective, for example, might become a target to increase the number of repeat donations to one in 50 first-time donors in a year, and one in 10 regular donors (who have already given more than once). You can make this target more realistic by looking at the current rates and then anticipating an increase. As an example, we have allocated yearly targets to each of the objectives listed above.

Using targets to meet specific objectives – examples

Objective: to increase the number of repeat donations

Year	*Target*
First-time donors:	
1	1 in 100 to give again within 12 months.
3	1 in 50 to give again within 12 months.
Donors who have given more than once:	
1	1 in 25 to give again within 12 months.
3	1 in 10 to give again within 12 months.

Objective: to increase the size of repeat donations

Year	*Target*
1	The average size of repeat donations should be equivalent to average previous donations.
3	The average size of repeat donations should be at least double the average size of previous donations.

Objective: to increase the number of donors giving in a more regular and committed way

Year	*Target*
1	5% of individual donors to participate in payroll giving.
3	10% of individual donors to participate in payroll giving.
3	5% of organisational donors to give support over a period of 12 months or more.

Objective: to involve donors more often in decision making

Year	*Target*
1	Survey all donors at least once during the year.
3	Survey all donors at least once during the year.
3	Involve 5% of donors in face to face meetings.
3	Set up a 'think tank' involving the top 10 organisational donors.

Objective: to involve donors more often in the group's activities

Year	*Target*
1	Hold two participatory events, specifically for donors.
3	Hold four participatory events, specifically for donors.
3	Invite regular donors to all other 'open' events.

Objective: to understand the profile of donors better

Year	*Target*
1	Analyse the database of donors, producing a report for trustees.
3	Produce an updated report for trustees.
3	Carry out a research project, looking into individual donors' priorities for the charity.

Objective: to find new donors, using data on existing donors as a guide

Year	*Target*
1	Increase the database of donors by 20% on the previous year.
3	increase the database of donors by 50% on the previous year.

Methodology

The next element in your plan should be an outline of the actions needed to realise your targets over the coming year.

Action list for realising targets – example

1. We will research and review our existing supporters.
2. We will use this information to research other possible funders.
3. We will continue an ongoing programme of PR to raise our profile in local, national and specialist media.
4. We will develop a timetable of mailings throughout the year.
5. We will carry out an annual survey of our donors.
6. We will develop a programme of contact events throughout the year.

You can also identify who will undertake these tasks, and how they relate to other fundraising and marketing activities.

Having worked out the various actions that are needed, you should have a clearer idea of the amount of time you need to spend looking after your donors. Your research into existing supporters, for example, might take you four or five days. Further research into other funders might take days or months, depending on the amount of fundraising you need to do during the year. It's fairly easy to work out how much time is involved in writing to donors, or in setting up contact events.

However, good relationships thrive on informal contact, as well as on formal meetings and mailings. So, once you have worked out your action plan (methodology) you might anticipate spending 30 days a year looking after your donors. In actual fact, when you take phone calls and informal meetings into account, you could be spending much more time on building up relationships with donors.

This doesn't make it easy to come up with an accurate budget for donor development. But it's important to set one.

Setting a budget

The first time you set a budget for the work involved in looking after your donors you will need to mix fairly accurate estimates with educated guesswork. Subsequent budgets will become easier, though never entirely scientific. The important thing to remember is that this budget is for your general 'customer care' activities. It is not for specific appeals and fundraising events. They will all have their own individual budgets with costs and expected income. This general customer care contributes to all the individual fundraising activities, but it's hard to put a figure on income directly raised as a result.

You might want to attribute any unsolicited donations to general customer care. But this won't be a true reflection of how much money has been raised through particular appeals, because of the ongoing contact with your donors.

Your budget might incorporate:

- time and overheads (based on the amount of time you think will be spent on general donor care, rather than specific appeals);
- computer costs (database software and maintenance);
- general mailings (newsletters, annual reports, anything which doesn't have a direct response – remember to include the cost of design, printing and postage);
- events and open days (allowing for hospitality, and venue costs if you are holding the event away from base);
- meetings (with travel expenses);
- other costs (you might want to produce certificates or plaques for your donors, for instance);
- contingency (it's always a good idea to have a small sum allocated for emergencies or the unexpected).

Building up donor numbers – a case study

A small community organisation put together a plan to try to build up the number of donors supporting the organisation. First they set themselves the following aims, objectives and targets, then they worked out their methodology and budget.

Aims

We would like to build a secure funding base for the organisation, by increasing the commitment of existing donors, and expanding our base of supporters.

Objectives and targets

1 To encourage repeat donations from our existing supporters.
Target: within three years we will secure repeat donations from at least a quarter of our first-time donors.

2 To expand our base of supporters.
Target: within three years we will double the number of donors on our database.

Methodology

Year 1

- We will review our existing database of supporters, filling in any gaps in the information.
- We will look at patterns in giving, and use this information to help us research other potential funders.
- We will develop three different leaflets, and send these to selected individuals on the database.
- We will send project updates and newsletters to relevant individuals and organisations on the database.

Timetable

Month 1:	Review of database
Month 2:	Research other funders
Months 3 and 9:	Newsletters
Months 4, 6 and 8:	Specialist mailings (payroll giving, annual report, Christmas catalogue)
Throughout the year:	Project updates

Budget

	£
Outgoings	
Time and overheads:	500
Computer costs:	300
Mailings (print, postage etc.):	2,000
Contingency:	200
Total:	3,000
Income	
Reserves:	1,000
Local authority:	300
Catalogue sales:	1,000
Total	2,300

(Remainder of income to be found across specific campaigns and appeals.)

We have already talked about the need to research and review existing supporters, and we are going to look at this in more detail in the next chapter.

3

Who are your donors?

Analysing your existing donors will help you contact them at the right times with appropriate information. It will enable you to see who are your key major donors – deserving special care and attention. It will help you to identify who else might support your cause. And it's important to go through this exercise at regular intervals, because things change.

Not only will you acquire new donors, but some will move, some will die, some will change their minds. And the mix of donors is likely to change. The number of trusts offering support may outweigh company donations at the moment. In two years' time the situation may be very different.

In this chapter we suggest some of the techniques you might use – for a first-time review, or a regular look at your donors.

The areas that we cover are:

- the need to identify who your donors are
- the importance of building relationships with individuals, even if it is their organisation signing the cheque
- how to map your donors, to get an idea of any emerging patterns
- the importance of identifying major donors, who need particular care and attention
- the need to keep accurate and up-to-date information on all of your donors
- the importance of complying with the Data Protection Act

The need to identify donors

If you are going to look after your donors effectively, developing your relationships with them, and building up their support, you need to understand them. Sometimes you can be working so closely with a small group of regular supporters that you don't see all the opportunities or patterns.

You might know almost every donor's name and personality. Even if you do, your colleagues can't be expected to have this level of knowledge. So, clearly identifying donors and logging all their details will provide a useful reference. In fact, your colleagues may well be dealing with these donors on other matters – quite unaware that they have provided financial support to your group in the past.

Equally, your colleagues might have some useful information, for instance about the likes and dislikes of particular donors, of which you are unaware.

Gathering all this information together allows you to create a donor profile. What you are doing at this stage is using all the knowledge your organisation already has on a donor. You are simply 'mapping' this out – collecting it together and storing it in one place so that it's easy to access and analyse. The 'How to' guide *Building a Fundraising Database Using your PC* (see *Further information*) gives more information on this topic. If you are storing information of this kind on individuals then it is vital to register with the Data Protection Registrar. We return to this issue on page 25.

Once you have mapped out the different types of donor, you will be able to develop communications and other support activities that are appropriate and targeted. You will also be able to approach your existing funders with relevant requests for further support.

Organisation or individual?

One of the first major distinctions to make, when looking at your donors, is between organisations and individuals.

Ultimately it's individuals within organisations who make decisions on whether or not to support your group or project. But they are working within rules or guidelines – there's room for discretion but not blatant favouritism.

Nevertheless, it is still important to build up your links with individuals within organisations – because people have to trust you and believe you will deliver the goods. Some organisations directly invite groups to apply to them for funding, and you would want to be one of those they remember to invite.

Individual donors vary a great deal in their motivation, patterns of giving and expectations. They can give in a wildly erratic way and no-one can criticise them for this. Having said this, most of us are creatures of habit and we're fairly predictable. So, it is worth trying to identify particular patterns – such as the time of year a person usually gives; which types of appeal they respond to; and how much they usually give. Many of your assumptions will turn out to be quite accurate. And this will enable you to raise more income by targeting your appeals more carefully.

On looking at its different funders over the years, a small charity realised that 10 of its 30 regular volunteers had originally made donations. They had been recruited after making their initial financial contribution. However, although they were asked to undertake a wide range of voluntary tasks – from driving and publicity through to practical environmental projects – they had never been asked for another donation. Only one of them had made any further financial contribution (and that was unprompted).

When the charity asked all 30 of its volunteers if they would like to make a regular or annual financial donation (in addition to their valuable donation of time and skills) over three quarters of them said 'yes'. They were approached personally by the director of the charity with the request.

Mapping your donors

How you go about the actual process of mapping your donors will depend on a variety of factors. Most importantly, it will depend on the size of your group, and on the number of people and organisations who are currently supporting your work.

If your funders are mostly organisations, then you could probably draw up a list to use as a basis for a full discussion with your colleagues. If, however, you have hundreds of individual donors, as well as organisational funders, you might want to hold a broad discussion/brainstorm session, to be followed by more detailed research and analysis carried out with the aid of a computer database.

Your brainstorm session could perhaps involve everyone from your organisation. In any case, it will certainly involve your trustees or management committee, and any of your colleagues who have PR, marketing or fundraising responsibilities.

One way to approach this activity is to draw up some large circles on flipchart paper – for example, one to represent individuals and one to represent organisations. Then you could divide these circles into sections like a pie chart.

Organisational donors

The different sections on the organisational chart might represent:

- statutory sources (Europe, national and local government, quangos);
- companies;
- trusts and foundations (including the National Lottery Charities Board);
- others (Rotary and Lions clubs, local schools and so on).

The chart showing how income is received from organisations would then look like this:

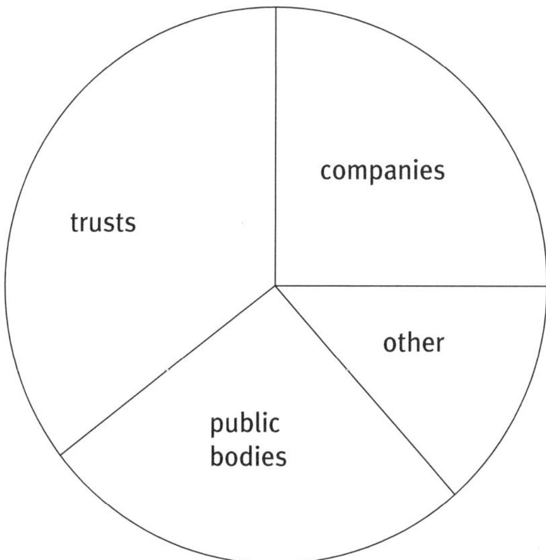

Individual donors

The circle representing individual donors might, for example, be subdivided into:

- mailing responses;
- collections (street/house-to-house);
- public appeals;
- events;
- membership;
- legacies.

The chart showing how income comes from individuals would then look like this:

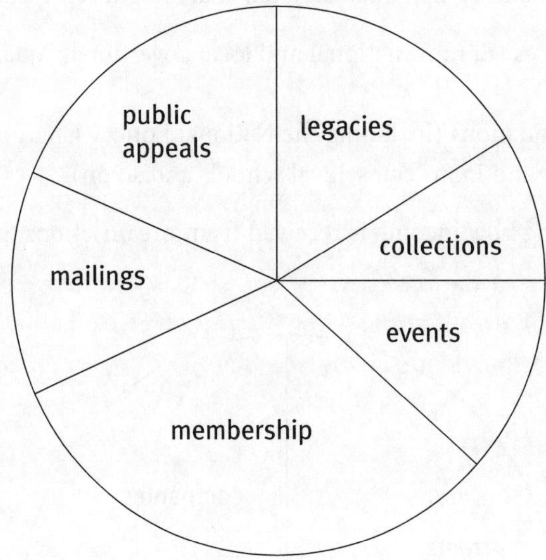

You might break down your individual donors into different categories, for example:

- young people;
- standard adult members;
- old age pensioners;
- life members.

The chart showing the categories of individual donors would then look like this:

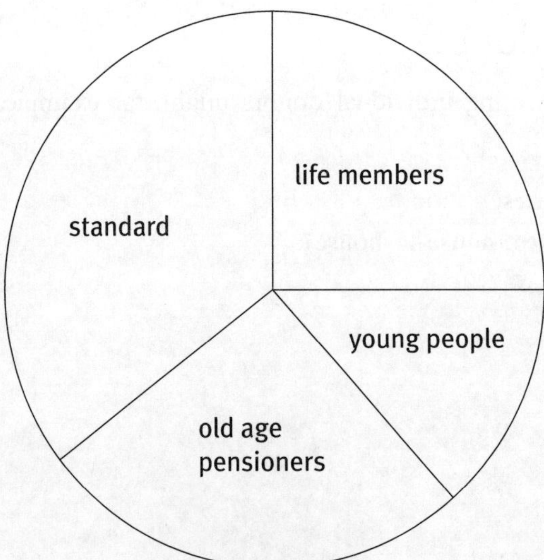

Once you have your flipchart (or other) diagrams of the different overall sources of income you are ready to focus in.

There are a number of questions you might ask at this stage, including:

- Who is in touch with these donors, for what reasons, and how often?
- Why do we think these donors give to us?
- How much are the different sub-divisions on the chart worth?
- Are there any patterns or gaps emerging?
- Are there any donors that we are heavily dependent on – who take up more than a quarter of the pie chart? If so, what would happen if they stopped supporting our organisation? How likely is that? And should we always be developing new big donors to replace them?

Who is in touch?

It can be quite revealing to look at who is in touch with your supporters. 'In touch' doesn't just mean contacting donors to ask for funds. It can also mean answering their telephone calls; sending them newsletters; accounting for their money; chairing meetings which they attend and so on.

It's important to consider the different people who are in touch, because they are all 'faces' of your group. They can all contribute as you try to raise more money from existing supporters.

It can be a useful exercise to work your way round the various diagrams attaching the names of people who are in contact with different types of donor – indicating the nature and frequency of contact.

Why your donors give

The next thing to ask is why people think the different types of donors support your work. You might have to keep this quite general if there are too many individuals and organisations to list. But it's still worth looking at each category and asking the question. It will help you to think about building up new support within the same categories. And it will give you an insight into why your donors give – and why they might give again.

You might think that certain companies support your organisation because, for example:

- they want to enhance their reputation locally and your organisation has a high profile;
- they have set up a company giving scheme to boost staff morale, and your projects are in the field of work which they want to support.

Trusts are set up to give money to particular good causes or beneficiaries, but you need to consider why they have chosen to give some of this money to you. How are you helping them to achieve their objectives?

Local government might have given you a grant to meet the needs of vulnerable people in the local community. But why choose your organisation? Is it because you offer value for money? Is it for some historical reason?

Individual giving is even more complicated. Many people give because they identify with a cause, and they believe in your work. Others are motivated by guilt or religion, many by some personal contact or experience. It might be easier to think about some types of donation than others. For example, someone who becomes a member of your group clearly has some affinity with your work. They believe in what you do and want to wear the badge, or display the bumper sticker. Someone giving to a street collection, however, simply happened to be in the right place, at the right time and in the right mood.

How much are they worth?

Another issue is how much the different sub-divisions are worth to your group. You can work this out in financial terms – for instance, trust support is worth £20,000 a year, and payroll giving is worth £1,000.

You might also like to think in terms of their more general value to your organisation – in developing new volunteers, demonstrating community support to potential trust funders, making small gifts now which could lead to a legacy in the future...

For example, you might get to know one or two companies by their support through gifts in kind. Financially gifts in kind might be worth £500 in any one year. But if they introduce you to companies who begin to trust you and want to support you in the future, the gift in kind could convert to a grant worth thousands in years to come. The ultimate value of gifts in kind can be much more than the simple first financial contribution. Critically, you should look in each of these sub-divisions and ask who are the major donors. Those giving the most support will need particular care and attention – possibly from your director or the chair of your trustees.

Identifying patterns and gaps

Once you have filled in as much detail as possible, you can stand back and look at the overall picture. You can ask, 'Are there any underlying patterns or obvious gaps?'

You might realise that people who respond to your direct mail don't have further contact with your group at the moment. Perhaps trusts which have given you small donations in the past appear more likely to give you a large grant than those you have not dealt with before. Possibly, there is an obvious gap – you might find you have no money coming from legacies or from events. You can then think about whether this is an area you would like to develop, or whether it is a deliberate gap.

Further research into existing donors

Hopefully, the audit will have given you some useful information on your overall funding mix, and levels of contact with supporters. As well as the general perspective you also need some detailed local information – to help you build up more of a profile on each donor.

You probably know quite a bit already. This will need to be recorded so that it can be referred to and analysed.

You are in regular communication with many of your donors – so you can ask them directly for some of the additional information you need. This might mean phoning organisations, or sending out a questionnaire to individuals. If you send out a questionnaire, state clearly how you intend to use the information. Offer respondents the chance to tick a box if they want the information to be restricted to your sole use (i.e. you won't sell it or pass it on for another organisation to use).

As far as organisations are concerned, there are many helpful directories and CDs available. See *Further information* for details.

What you will find essential is a computer database. You can buy specially designed packages for charity fundraisers. Suppliers regularly advertise in *Third Sector* magazine (see *Further information*). If you have less money to hand but do have a PC with Windows, you can set up your own fairly powerful database.

You might want to make a huge effort to gather a lot of information in one go, followed by gradual amendments and additions. Or you might want to go for a slow and steady build up. The important thing is to think it through at the outset so that you gather the same sort of information on all your donors. If you aren't clear and consistent you will have to keep going back to ask for more information.

Two groups based in the same community centre compared notes on the sort of information they stored on their donors. One – a very small newly-formed charity – held the following details:

Name;
Type of donor (individual or organisation);
Organisation (if applicable);
Job title;
Address;
Telephone number;
Donations (listed by date);
Correspondence (indicating whether or not a thank-you letter had been sent, for instance).

The other held much more information on each donor:

Name;
Type of donor (individual or organisation);
Organisation (if applicable);
Job title;
Address;
Telephone number;
Donations (listed by date, and categorised according to the method of payment and the appeal responded to);
Funding preferences (this information had been completed for both individuals and organisations and was regularly updated);
Mailings (here they indicated whether or not the donor should be sent newsletters, annual reports, catalogues and so on);
Notes (in this area they listed previous conversations or observations).

Keeping track of donors

Once you have information on your donors it's vital to keep the details up to date. If people die or move on you need to know, and you need to amend your records accordingly – at the very least to avoid embarrassment and upset.

If a trust changes its funding priorities you need to make a note so that you can contact them with appropriate proposals. If a council grants officer changes jobs, you need details so that you are introduced to their replacement, and so that you can stay in touch with them in their new role.

In other words, you should carry out an annual database update, or work out some other mechanism to keep the information topical – by including an address update sheet with your newsletters, for example.

A community centre received a large donation from a trust five years ago. However, the details of the grant were not entered on the organisation's donor database. The community centre approached the trust asking for a similar amount of money, making no reference to the previous donation. When the trust's representative rang the centre, the new manager was extremely embarrassed to discover that funding had been given in the past. The trust had a policy of not funding similar projects from the same organisation.

Databases and data protection

The information you hold on individuals will allow you to contact the appropriate people at the right time, and to send them appeals that suit their personal preferences and attitudes.

All information held about 'living identifiable people' is governed by the Data Protection Act 1998 (which replaces the Data Protection Act 1984).

The new Act is coming into force at the time of writing. For up-to-date information check with the office of the Data Protection Registrar (see *Further information*). You will also find useful information in *Data Protection for Voluntary Organisations* (see *Further information*).

The new Act will retain the principles of good practice enshrined in the original legislation. These principles include a need for information to be processed 'fairly and lawfully'. To meet this requirement you must inform the person who is the subject of your data of the identity of the 'data controller' and tell them why the data is being processed.

You will only be allowed to process information if:

- the individual has given their consent to the processing;
- the processing is necessary for the performance of a contract with the individual;
- the processing is required under a legal obligation;
- the processing is necessary to protect the vital interest of the individual or to carry out public functions;
- the processing is necessary in order to pursue the legitimate interest of the data controller or certain third parties (unless prejudicial to the interests of the individual).

It is good practice to get a donor's permission to record and use their data the first time you communicate with them. Many organisations include a brief explanation of how the person's details might be used and then ask respondents to tick a box if they don't want to receive further mailings, or if they don't want their details passed on to third parties. You are asking people to opt out, rather than to opt in. Keep a copy of any such forms you receive back for reference.

If you have any worries in this area, then contact the office of the Data Protection Registrar. At all times state clearly how information will be used – providing people with the opportunity to opt out.

Looking forward

Armed with all this information on your donors and complying with the Data Protection Act you will be ready to build new, strong relationships with your donors.

You will also be able to look into potential donors – first-time supporters. This is the focus of our next chapter.

4

Researching potential donors

Once you have an idea of who currently supports your organisation you can go out and approach other potential donors. Although it can cost up to five times more to raise money from a new donor, you need to spend some of your resources reaching new supporters. If you don't then your income could shrink over time as people choose to give their money to different charities, and as organisations change their funding policies.

In this chapter we look at:

- The need to continue to recruit new donors
- How to use information on your existing donors to target your efforts to find new donors
- How to make use of your networks to reach new donors
- Using other resources and support to find information on organisations and individuals

Fitting in with your fundraising plan

Any research into new donors must fit within the aims and direction given by your organisation's fundraising plan. There's no point in building up a pile of information on company giving if your fundraising plan is clear that you will be raising most money from trusts, council contracts and community donations.

Similarly, there is no need to put a huge effort into building up information on new individual donors if your current supporters give a steady, predictable income which already meets the demands of your fundraising plan.

New donors versus repeat donations

So, there is a balance needed between your work with existing donors and potential donors.

New donors offer:

- potentially larger untapped sums of money;
- enthusiasm for your cause (not exhaustion);
- new ideas;
- a chance to spread any risks (if some of your existing donors stop supporting you).

On the other hand new donors:

- are hard to find (and your success rate in appeals will be lower);
- have to be won over;
- might start with a small contribution and gradually build up to a larger one;
- might have loyalties to other causes.

Existing donors offer:

- loyalty, and they are easier to win over (they are 'warm prospects');
- the potential to build a regular, dependable commitment;
- more likelihood of a larger contribution (because they trust you);
- many added benefits (from being advocates on your behalf through to introducing you to other funders).

However, existing donors:

- might tire of your appeals, and you will lose a certain percentage each year;
- have limited resources between them (you won't be able to grow if you don't expand your donor base);
- need regular contact to keep them happy, informed and involved (costing you resources).

There's a lot to be gained, then, from both new and existing donors. And information on existing donors is a good starting point for research into new donors.

Building on existing information

In the last chapter we saw that the information you build up on your donors can reveal particular patterns or gaps. This is a good starting point for any research into new donors.

Look at your individual supporters and consider where they live, what sort of job they do (if appropriate), how old they are and whether they're male or female (it might be relevant). You might discover that a particular local area is well or badly represented. If it's well represented, you might want to develop donations from existing supporters (or encourage them to raise money from friends and neighbours). If it's badly represented you might want to do some general public relations work there, before making an appeal for funds. You might look at the socio-economics of the area. If it's a relatively poor, disadvantaged area, you might feel that it's not appropriate to try to raise money there. If the area is dominated by businesses rather than households, this will affect the type of fundraising you do locally.

If a large number of your donors work for a particular company, this might be the result of an appeal having been circulated within their organisation. You might want to repeat this with another employer. If most of your supporters seem to be women you might try to redress the balance by targeting men (with a specially designed leaflet). Alternatively, you might decide women are more likely to support your work, so you will continue to concentrate on them.

The information you have on organisational donors can be equally revealing. Companies from a particular industry or location might make up the bulk of your corporate supporters. It makes sense to think about whether there's an obvious link that makes your work attractive. Before firing off appeals to similar companies you need to consider how your existing supporters will feel if their rivals start to become associated with your organisation too.

These are just a few examples of how you can work from knowledge of existing donors and think about new opportunities. The key is to build on your information in a sensitive way. You have gathered some very helpful intelligence. It's up to you to use it wisely.

Using your networks

You are in touch with a number of different people and organisations who can all help you to reach new donors.

As well as looking at your donors to see what sort of person or organisation supports you, you can work with them to find new funders. You might also work in similar ways with your volunteers, colleagues and other contacts, for instance:

- You might benefit from their **knowledge** – asking them if they know anyone or any organisation that might be interested in your work.
- Some of your contacts might introduce or **recommend** you directly to another potential donor.
- You might give details of some of your current supporters as **references** when approaching other people.
- You might ask some funders, colleagues and friends to **fundraise** on your behalf with their own contacts.

A small community centre had a sudden need to raise £3,000 for a small repair to the building. The centre had only recently raised £40,000 from a public appeal. The director didn't want to ask the same donors for more money just a month later. So, she approached the 10 largest individual supporters from the recent appeal, and asked them if they would like to raise funds on the centre's behalf. Nine of them agreed. The tenth wrote out a cheque for £300 immediately.

The centre director provided each of the supporters with information about how the local community benefits from the centre, plus photographs showing how the building had already been improved.

The nine donors each raised their £300 within six weeks. They were enthusiastic advocates, and they used a mix of face-to-face fundraising and coffee mornings to raise money. One made a sponsored bike ride.

All of the fundraisers provided the centre with details of the people who had made donations. These were added to the centre's database. They were thanked for their contribution, and the centre kept in touch – anticipating more donations in the future.

External sources of information

Once you have exhausted your own sources of information (your existing database, and information from friends, supporters and colleagues) you will need to look for details from external sources.

In addition to the sources mentioned below, *Find the Funds* in this series (see *Further information*) gives more advice on researching and finding the best places to fundraise.

Directories, databases and CD-ROMs

If you are trying to build up information on different organisations who might make donations then there are various directories and CD-ROMs to help – details are given in *Further information*.

The important point here is that these directories and databases are reference tools. They are not mailing lists. You should work through them to find out specific information, to discover the matches between the work you do and the areas the organisation wants to fund.

When it comes to individual donors you can find out the names of all adults living at a particular address from the Electoral Roll – you can consult the Roll in public libraries. Different companies also make their mailing lists available (sometimes at a substantial price). You can find out about available mailing lists by contacting the Direct Marketing Association (listed in *Further information*).

Reciprocal mailing

If you are involved in regular direct mail campaigns you might also want to consider the use of what are called 'reciprocal mailings'. This can involve contacting your supporters with an appeal on behalf of a complementary organisation – explaining why you think it might be of interest. And they will do the same for you with their donors. This arrangement can bring you into contact with new supporters. But it needs careful handling: to ensure you stay within the rules of the Data Protection Act; to avoid upsetting your existing donors or exhausting their pockets; and to prevent confusion or mixed messages. The object is to build additional support not to lose current donors.

Development and advice agencies

You might be able to find out about particular local organisations or philanthropists through development or advice agencies. These include rural community councils, councils of community/voluntary service, volunteer bureaux, charity information bureaux and local authority external funding officers. Details of such groups will usually be found in the telephone directory or in your local library.

Many of these agencies will have funding databases and directories which you can use for reference. They might be able to provide some useful hints too. And they might know of particular local family trusts or generous individuals living nearby.

Fundraising groups

Rotary clubs, the Round Table, Lions clubs, Soroptomists and other local fundraising groups can also be useful sources of information (as well as funds!). They might be able to point you in the direction of particular people and organisations with an interest in your area of work.

Consultants

There are a number of fundraising consultants who can advise and carry out research on your behalf. Many are members of the Institute of Charity Fundraising Managers (ICFM). Members of ICFM adhere to particular principles and good practice guidelines.

Fundraising consultants are there to support you. Don't expect to simply hand over whole projects to them, and wait for them to come back with the money six months later. It doesn't work like that. Consultants can help you to draw up a list of potential donors, and work with you to devise campaigns and appeals. Ultimately the request for money needs to come from you.

Additional research

Once you have exhausted all the other sources of fundraising information on potential donors, there is still more that you can do. You can do your own digging.

Ringing organisations

Your reference library will have lists of local businesses, compiled by organisations such as the council's economic development unit. Of course, businesses are also listed in the telephone directory and *Yellow Pages*. You can make contact with organisations that sound promising and ask them for information on their charitable donations, or funding policies. You can ask for copies of their annual reports to see how they spent their money last year.

You can make similar contact with local government, quangos and trusts to build up more information about their approach to funding groups like yours. It's always worth getting as much detail as possible at this stage to avoid wasted mailings and false hope when you send a request for funding.

Monitoring media coverage

It's also useful to monitor the local paper, or even parish and local authority magazines, for any mention of donations to good causes. You can start to build up an idea of what these organisations have funded already, and where their sympathies lie.

The local press might also contain details on gifts from individuals, so it's worth keeping a cuttings file.

Using the Internet

Increasingly fundraisers are using the Internet to help with their research – either through their own access to the web, or by using computers in libraries, cyber cafés or development agencies. You can find out information on organisations that have a website – searching for particular key words, reading their annual reports online and so on. You might also develop your own website, asking people who visit to provide you with details of their e-mail addresses. This way you can build up an e-mail list of people who have an interest in your work, and who can be sent very targeted appeals.

Contacting solicitors

Firms of solicitors are also worth approaching. They might administer small, well-hidden, family trusts. They might be responsible for a will where the person has asked quite generally for their money to be given to 'local good causes'.

Even if the solicitors don't look after any trusts you might want to give details of your organisation in case anyone is making a will and wants a 'good cause' to nominate.

Contacting funeral directors

Similarly, you might want to give your details to local funeral directors, so that when families ask for donations rather than flowers, your group is recommended to them. This is something that a number of charities have done in recent years. Ultimately, the decision is down to the family concerned.

A cancer support group provided its details to all firms of funeral directors in the county in which it is based. The charity sent leaflets giving details of its service and explaining specifically how a donation of between £10 and £20 would be used (the sort of sum of money often spent on flowers). In the past three years, 10 families have asked for donations to be made to the charity, in place of flowers. In nine cases, the death concerned was from cancer.

Active research

You might want to build up your list of potential donors by running a competition or holding an event. This is quite an active way of reaching new funders. A competition tempts them to give you information in return for a decent prize. An event gives you the chance to demonstrate your work in action whilst finding out more about them (it's both personal and engaging).

5

Repeat donations – an overview

As we saw in the last chapter, approaching new donors or 'cold calling' often involves quite a lot of research, and your success rates can be relatively low, with increased fundraising costs for every pound you raise. Nurturing your existing donors can be highly productive.

In this chapter we provide an overview of some of the issues and opportunities, before focusing on repeat donations from organisations and, then, from individuals.

We look at:

- The need to raise your profile generally
- How to strike the right balance – asking for the right amount at the right time
- How to develop your relationship into a win-win situation
- The importance of keeping a record of all your donor development work
- Being clear about when you are asking for funds, and what you are asking for
- Developing a system of customer care to deal with enquiries, complaints and offers of support

Public relations and marketing

Your overall programme of PR and marketing is as important to your existing donors as it is to potential supporters.

A good profile

Anything that you do to raise the profile of your organisation will help to make your current donors feel good about supporting you. Seeing your name in the news will help to reassure them that they made the right decision in giving you money. And hearing about the other things you have planned might prompt them to give again.

Research by Henley Management College revealed that the most important factor, when it comes to making a charitable donation, is that organisation's reputation. On a scale of one to five, this was rated 3.99. Other factors rated three or more out of five were: the charity spends a high proportion of income on its cause; the charity is managed professionally; and the charity is seen to make a real impact on its cause. All of these factors can be addressed through a strong and positive public profile.

Publicity on specific campaigns

It is important to publicise specific fundraising achievements. People who have given money to a particular project will want to know that their contribution has made a difference.

A children's health charity received some good publicity for its fundraising campaign. The charity had raised £13,000 for a project delivering training and information to health professionals, schools, and youth and community services. The local paper had covered the launch of the campaign, reported on progress – when the charity passed the halfway mark, and when the full amount had been raised.

In the week after the final article appeared, the charity received unsolicited donations from individuals worth a further £500. It was contacted by a school that wanted the training and information, but also wanted to raise money on the charity's behalf. And a local printing company offered to design and print the information leaflets free of charge.

We are going to look at publicity opportunities in more detail below, and there is further advice in the 'How to' guide on *Effective Media Relations* and in *The DIY Guide to Public Relations* (see *Further information*).

Not asking for too much or too often

On the one hand you need to keep your organisation in people's minds (through PR and marketing), on the other you don't want to overload them with information and requests for money.

You need to try not to ask for too much, too often.

How much is too much? How often is too often? There's no single answer. What is appropriate for one donor will not be right for another. So, it is worth putting some sort of codes into your database. These can indicate how often someone should be contacted and what level of funding or type of appeal they might be interested in.

The danger of asking for too much is that a donor simply can't give such a sum, and instead of giving a smaller amount they give nothing at all. The problem with asking too often is that it can seem greedy and put people off your organisation altogether. People might feel you are spending too much on appeals.

Don't let this prevent you from keeping in touch though, because you can send people reports, newsletters and other information. You don't always have to be asking directly for money, as we shall see in the following chapters. When you do make appeals, these can vary and make use of some creative and unusual approaches to keep people interested.

Research in America has shown that each time you send out an appeal you will receive a response from about 10% of those you write to. But who responds will vary. Some will give every time. Others will respond if their personal circumstances allow or if they are particularly interested. People have different sums of money available at different times, and you can't know who will respond positively. They might not respond because they are on holiday, are ill, or have lost your mailing, for instance. Mailing more often can increase your chances of securing a donation from a particular individual.

Creating win-win situations

When you build up your relationships with donors you should be aiming for 'win-win' situations. This means that it's not just you benefiting from the relationship – your funders must get something out of it too.

We saw in the introduction to this guide that you can gain some tremendous benefits from your committed donors. But what do they get out of the relationship?

They might get:

- a sense of pride from supporting your work;
- good publicity for themselves/their organisation (and a better reputation);
- the opportunity to make a difference in the community.

If you can ask yourself 'What would make donor X feel like they were a win-win funder?', then you might come up with some good ideas that work with them and with other supporters.

An environmental charity had a broad range of donors – from multinational companies through to individual children. When the fundraiser asked himself the 'win-win' question he came up with satisfactory answers for all of the group's supporters. However, he felt that the charity could do more for its younger donors.

So, he developed a 'Green Patrol' club for those aged 11 and under, and a 'Small World' club for 12–16 year olds. Through club newsletters and a section of the charity's website the young people received information and ideas on the environment. The club was extended to children who hadn't made a donation before – they paid a subscription to join.

Your donors as advocates

When you think about your side of the 'win-win' situation you probably focus on the money that's coming in, and the predictability of this income. But it's important to remember that you can benefit in other ways – particularly when your supporters act as advocates or ambassadors on your behalf.

You can sit back and hope that people are going out there saying nice things about you. You can also be a bit more active, and encourage people or give them the tools they need.

One way of doing this is to ask that your newsletters are passed on to another reader (to spread your message). Perhaps you can ask that your newsletter is passed on to the local dental or doctor's surgery (to be read by many more people).

You might put a small message on any appeal letters or thank-you notes, asking your donor to tell a friend about your work.

Another thing you could do is to produce some literature for people to distribute, or invite your supporters to buy your Christmas cards to send to their friends (with your message included).

You need to think about how you could help people to be more active advocates of your group.

You might even want them to do some local fundraising for you. If you do ask for this sort of help you need to provide adequate support; in the form of advice, materials and encouragement.

A self-help group for people with mental health problems wanted to reach more people in the local community – and build up its membership. The group had a small base of individual donors and support from five key organisations. It provided its individual funders with car bumper stickers with a message from the group and a contact phone number. All members also had such stickers. Organisations were sent small posters to display around their offices or centres – again carrying a simple message and phone number.

The membership drive attracted 12 new members within the first three months, and is still reaching new people all the time.

The funders who took part were very actively involved in helping the group reach out into new parts of the local community. There was a real sense of achievement. And so the group is now planning a more ambitious awareness-raising campaign involving all of its donors.

Managing your information

However ambitious you are, and whatever you do to nurture your donors, you need to record what you are up to and share this information with colleagues.

Some of the key information will need to be put into your database – saying when you last contacted a donor, what you said or sent them and so on. Other information might be stored in a rigorous (and obvious) filing system.

It's absolutely vital to record and manage such information, otherwise most of your efforts will be wasted. If you find out that a particular organisation loves your newsletter, but only wants to be asked for money once a year when it has its donations committee meeting – note that. Don't include it in regular mailings, or even special appeals that fall outside this time.

Making sure you ask!

When you are approaching people for money don't be too subtle. When you are seeking support say so. Many people get embarrassed about the actual asking. But you need to be direct, and make it easy for people to respond.

If you want an irregular but frequent donor to consider payroll giving, make sure you ask them; don't just hope they'll realise it's a good idea (even if you send them an explanatory leaflet).

If you don't ask directly, this is like leaving the return address off your appeal literature.

So be clear about why you are communicating with your donor. If it's to keep them informed and happy, then that's one thing. If it's specifically to raise funds – then ask!

A charity for older people sent a letter to all of its supporters urging them to look at the enclosed leaflet – describing an important new project. The leaflet outlined a plan to build a sensory garden for blind people. The leaflet said how much the group needed to raise and by when. It had a picture of what the garden might look like. It quoted some blind people, saying how much the garden would improve their lives. Nowhere did it ask for contributions (although it did give a return address!). The mailing prompted a few people to make donations, but it didn't raise nearly enough.

A local Lions Club got to hear about the project and, after discussions with the charity, raised the remainder of the money. It was a fortunate intervention. But it might not have been needed if the original mailing had included a request for funding, and perhaps a reply slip with suggested amounts with tick boxes beside them.

Customer care

Looking after your donors doesn't just mean keeping them informed, finding out more about them and asking for additional donations (which is all about you being proactive). It's also about providing customer care when you react to approaches by your donors.

You need to have a clear system for dealing with written or telephone enquiries made by your donors. We have already seen that donors come into contact with different people or 'different faces' of your organisation. You will want to ensure that all these contacts are positive.

You might want to brief colleagues about some of your largest and most regular donors, so that they understand their importance. Colleagues should all know how to get into your donor database if they want to find out about a particular individual or organisation. And all callers should be treated as if they are important supporters.

If a donor rings with an enquiry, and you are unavailable, it is essential for their details to be noted, and for them to be treated in a positive, friendly manner. If people don't have the appropriate information, then the worst thing they can do is to try to answer a query with an inaccurate response.

You might want to run some training sessions with colleagues to ensure calls and queries are handled as you would expect.

Occasionally people will be unhappy or confused about something, and they might ring or write to complain. Such problems need to be dealt with effectively or you will lose this donor. Again, a polite and friendly manner is essential. Whoever receives the enquiry should make a note of the complaint and give a realistic time within which the caller will be rung back.

It's vital to keep this promise. If the issue is one of confusion, then you might want to ring and then clarify things in writing. If there is a genuine problem, then you need to discuss this with your donor and see if things can be sorted out to their satisfaction. If your organisation has made a mistake, accept responsibility gracefully. Don't try to make excuses. Explain how things will be put right.

Hopefully, problems will be few and far between. But it's good to be prepared. If you treat your donors well, they will be more likely to repeat their donations. They might even call when you are out to offer support – you will want to have a system in place to be able to respond positively!

6

Benefiting again from organisations

Many organisations are quite cautious when they support a charity for the first time. So, you might find that your first contact with a grant-making trust or a company is through a small donation, or perhaps support in kind (the gift of a product or service).

As they get to know and trust you, many organisations will be more generous and more creative about how they are prepared to support your work.

In this chapter we look at:

- The different types of contribution an organisation might make to your work
- How to gradually develop the type of support you receive from organisations
- How to develop a project in partnership with an organisation
- Other ways in which you can benefit from an organisation

Progress from small and low-risk to larger funding

You might like to think of support from organisations as layers in a pyramid. The bottom layer might include the smallest contributions in straight financial terms – gifts in kind, small-scale advertising and one-off small donations. Move up a level and you might include larger donations, sponsorship and secondments. Towards the top you might find large, long-term funding (over three to five years), partnership working, and service-level agreements – see the diagram overleaf:

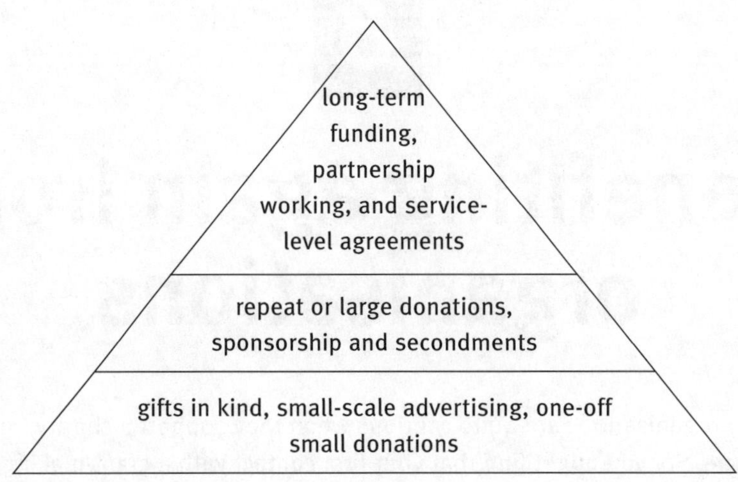

The width of each layer of the pyramid represents the numbers of different organisations likely to support you at each level. At the bottom you will find it relatively easy to secure small donations and gifts in kind from organisations. They might never have supported your group before. But, if you raise your profile so that they have heard about you, and if you demonstrate how you will put their contributions to good use, you might convince them to provide some support. Large-scale and long-term funding is much rarer; that's why we've put it at the top of the pyramid.

Some companies, trusts and public bodies will move through this pyramid, supporting you in different ways. And if they want to take few risks with their money, they may well start at the foot of the pyramid and work their way up.

This all assumes that the organisations have access to sufficient funding. Unfortunately, many community groups will be only too aware that local authorities, in particular, have been cutting back the money they make available – unless it is for service-level agreements (where you are, in effect, fulfilling a contract for them). Even if you have the best relationship possible with a council, it can't support you if the resources are not there. But if you have worked closely and stayed in touch, it might make more efforts to peg your funding at current levels, or help you find alternative sources of support.

So, it's important to be realistic about what you can achieve by nurturing your organisational donors. They don't have open-ended cheque books. The opportunity for repeat and increased donations will be governed by available budgets.

But there is still a lot that you can do. It might mean that organisations that have given you small donations in the past can be approached for further small contributions, or slightly larger donations. It might mean that organisations that have given you large project funding in the past can be approached for smaller-scale support. Some organisations will have sufficient budgets to move from gifts in kind, or loans, through to long-term rolling funding, or repeat donations.

You can look after all of your organisational donors in some of the ways that we describe in the following chapters. What will vary, though, will be the ways you approach them for repeat funding, and what you ask of them. Each of these approaches will need to be tailored to reflect your relationship, their funding in the past, their funding policies and their current financial circumstances.

A charity working to support economic regeneration in the local community received support from a range of organisations and individuals. Recently it had successfully applied to three trusts for small donations. Each of these donations supported different community-led projects: one funded a clean-up of a shared play area, one funded a short literacy scheme and one supported a young people's video project.

The charity kept in touch with all trusts in very similar ways throughout the three projects, building good relationships with administrators and trustees. One trust was a large national funder and it went on to fund a literacy development worker's post over three years. Another was a small family trust with limited resources. The trust said that it would be willing to fund other projects at the same level in the future. The final trust had a policy of not giving to the same organisation until at least three years after its original grant.

Pilot projects and feasibility

One of the ways you might begin a relationship with an organisation is to ask for its support with a pilot project or for a feasibility study. The risks involved are relatively low for both you and your funder. However, such development projects can produce valuable information for you to build on. And at the same time you will be making a strong case for repeat or expanded funding.

Your backer has bought into the idea at a very early stage – perhaps with little evidence of the need. By the end of your pilot study, though, you will be armed with statistics and suggested ways forward. You will be able to prove to your funder that it invested wisely. The organisation might be persuaded to support the next phase too.

A charity for children with learning difficulties was offered accommodation within a company's premises for its pilot holiday play scheme. Over the three-week play scheme the charity invited staff from the host company to take part in some activities and a play scheme party. At the end of the play scheme the charity reviewed its effectiveness and began to plan for an expanded scheme the following year. The host company offered accommodation and additional funding.

Of course, not all pilot projects succeed. And you don't embark on a pilot project purely to hook a funder with a small contribution, before asking for more. You might even decide that whilst your funder is happy and wants the initiative to continue, you don't believe it should develop in the same way. It's essential to be honest with your funder about the outcomes and potential ways forward.

Partnership working

There are various ways for your relationship to develop with a funder. You might come up with 101 different ideas, projects and developments – each time approaching a donor for support. But you might develop a genuinely fruitful partnership with a funder – where it can suggest new approaches that it wants to support which fit in with your aims and objectives.

If a funder sits on various project committees such a partnership is more likely to grow. It will only work if the funder has a thorough understanding of your goals, and if you provide the opportunities to think creatively and with no obligation.

A group set up to improve disabled people's access to employment opportunities received funding for its helpline from a local council's social inclusion unit. An officer from this unit sat on the group's advisory committee. At one of the meetings, the committee was looking at ways of raising employers' awareness of the Disability Discrimination Act and other issues. The council representative suggested a conference, and offered to part-fund it, with the balance of money coming from delegate fees. The group welcomed the suggestion and ran a successful conference. At the same time the social inclusion unit of the council was able to demonstrate that it had made a contribution in this important area – meeting one of the local authority's priorities for the year.

Different projects

Sometimes funders see only a small part of your organisation, and don't know about other aspects of your work. It may be that if they were aware of these other projects, or areas, they might want to support them.

It is therefore important to keep your funders posted on everything that is going on, introducing them to colleagues and their work, and letting them know what is planned. There's a delicate balance to be struck between making sure the donors are aware of everything you do, and overburdening them with too much information. But, just because a funder has traditionally supported one area of your work, don't assume it won't want to know about another. It might just have been a matter of luck or timing that it has ended up contributing to a particular project.

An environmental charity worked in a range of areas – in schools (providing information and projects), in industry (offering advice on the reduction of waste and recycling) and with the general public (providing an advisory telephone service). One of the charity's funders – a large company – had made a number of donations to support the work of providing advice to the general public. It had also paid for a research project, exploring ways of improving its own environmental performance.

The company's community affairs officer was in regular contact with the charity's manager of the public helpline and the employers' liaison officer. They met for one-to-one meetings, often spoke on the phone and met at different networking events. It wasn't until the community affairs officer attended the charity's annual general meeting that she became aware of the charity's work in schools. The company's marketing department had recently made educational sponsorship a priority, but had already allocated the budget for the year. So, this was a missed opportunity for the environmental charity!

Non-cash donations

We have already seen that non-cash donations can be a good way for an organisation to become initially involved in supporting your work at little or no cost or risk to itself. Such support can also be a valuable extension of an organisation's contribution to your work.

It might even be a way of building a closer relationship with your funders – particularly if you get involved in something like a skills exchange.

A skills exchange can bring you closer to an organisation and give each of you a better understanding of how the other works. One of your volunteers or members of staff swaps places with one of the organisation's employees. Alternatively, you might sit on each other's committees – adding a new perspective drawn from different experiences.

Staff giving

Don't forget that even if you have exhausted the organisation's budget, its staff might do their own fundraising. It's worth finding out whether there is a staff scheme. The organisation might have a staff fundraising committee that you can talk to. They might get involved in payroll giving.

A children's hospice received a large donation from a local company. The company gave the money it had won in an industrial competition. It didn't usually have such sums to give away, as it was quite a small organisation. The company told all staff about the contribution, and the hospice made a presentation at the company's quarterly staff meeting. The staff wanted to continue to support the work of the hospice and set up a staff fundraising committee especially to do so.

All it takes is imagination and realism

The above ideas are just some of the ways in which you can benefit again from your organisational donors. There are many more – and you are limited only by your imagination and what organisations can realistically afford or do.

In the next few chapters we look at some of the techniques to build up your relationships with organisational donors: keeping them informed, showing them your work, involving them in decisions, and giving them sufficient credit.

7

Keeping organisations informed

People have short memories. And when they're busy they won't be thinking about your group and the work you do. So, it's important to keep them informed: to remind them that you exist, and to keep them feeling good about you. You can do this in a variety of ways, as we explain in this chapter.

We cover:

- The difference between 'regular' and 'often' when thinking about ways of staying in touch
- The role of public relations in developing relationships with organisations
- How to secure publicity, and in which media
- What kind of information organisations need or want
- Different ways of providing the information

Regular contact

One of the ways to remain in people's minds is by contacting them regularly. 'Regularly' is not the same as 'often'. You might make contact with someone just once or twice in a year, but if this is planned and consistent then this is 'regular'.

Your contact can be a simple phone call, it might be a letter, a project report or a face-to-face meeting... We are going to run through some of these ways of staying in touch below. The important point to make here, though, is that you need to plan for regular contact, and what is right for one organisation will not be appropriate for another. So, you will need to record these differences on your database.

It's a bit like an advertising sales-person's database or card index system. They usually have three or four categories of organisation in their system – A, B, C and D. The As get calls once a fortnight, because they advertise frequently and might need a quick prompt or simply a call to say 'hello, how are you'. The Bs are rung once a month, because they advertise less frequently, but usually a couple of times a year. The Cs are called every two or three months because they advertised last year. And the Ds might be rung once a year to see if they are interested in advertising again – even though it's quite some time since they last did so. Just imagine if that sales-person rang the D category organisations once a fortnight – the Ds would get extremely fed-up!

Public relations

PR is another way of staying in people's minds. It's less direct than personal contact, but it can also be more subtle. It also seems like an endorsement – because if what you're doing is good enough to get reported in the papers and on radio it must be fairly worthwhile.

What is important is working out the relevant papers, magazines, radio and television programmes to target. You won't necessarily get coverage in all of them, but it would be pointless sending information to the local newspaper in a remote area if all of your organisational donors are based in London, or if they all read a particular funders' magazine.

Your PR will be serving a variety of purposes, so you will be putting together a database of media to reflect the different audiences you want to reach, including:

- existing donors;
- potential donors;
- staff and volunteers;
- clients, customers, or users;
- key decision makers;
- others as appropriate.

In this context, PR will help show existing donors what they have helped to achieve through their support, and it might reveal other potential funding opportunities.

Who to target

But how do you know the appropriate media to target for your organisational donors?

You could ask them, of course. You might send out a questionnaire, or simply ask some different funders who you think are representative of their particular area.

You might look in a media directory such as *Benn's*. This directory categorises different publications under headings such as 'local government', 'charities' and specific industrial sectors, for instance 'catering industry'. Details are provided in *Further information.*

As well as considering the specialist publications, remember that funders listen to the radio and watch the main television channels too. It's harder to get publicity on these channels, but it's worth having a go. And if you know in advance that you're going to be featured on *Woman's Hour*, for instance, then you might want to send a quick note to some key funders so that they definitely switch on!

A mental health charity's director was interviewed for a national television documentary, exploring depression in older people. The production company that made the programme printed some promotional postcards advertising the documentary. The charity sent out 100 of these cards to its largest organisational donors to ensure they saw the programme (or if they didn't watch it, to appreciate that the charity was featured on prime time television).

What to publicise

The sorts of things that you might want to publicise to organisational donors include:

- project successes or milestones;
- fundraising successes;
- forthcoming events/activities;
- surveys/evidence of need;
- opportunities to get involved/provide support.

How to get publicity

You might be approached by the media to take part in a programme, or to make a comment on something topical. But, if you want to announce something that you think is newsworthy then it will be down to you to make the approach.

In this case, you will need to write a news release and send it to the appropriate media. You will find advice on how to do this in the 'How to' guide *Effective Media Relations* and in *The DIY Guide to Public Relations* (see *Further information*).

Your news release should be written in simple, short, punchy sentences. You should begin with the main point of your news release – for example:

- 'The Mill Road Charity has raised £5,000 for its new day centre.'
- 'A survey by The Mill Road Charity shows that over 30% of older people locally leave their homes just once a week or less.'

Your news release needs to have a heading that obviously reflects the content that follows. And you need to give contact details so that journalists can find out more.

It's a good idea to include a quote – from your director or someone who has benefited from your charity.

What do your organisational donors want to know?

Your publicity can reflect different aspects of your work, and these will be more or less interesting to your organisational funders. However, when it comes to more direct contact you need to ensure you are telling them about things that will definitely be of interest.

Few organisations will want to know that you have appointed a new administrative assistant unless they've provided funding for the post. But they might want to know about the appointment of a new director or trustee.

So, what might they be interested in? Here are some suggestions, but you will need to come up with your own list to meet the needs and personalities of your different funders:

- project successes – particularly if they are involved in a particular project;
- fundraising successes – especially if they have contributed to an appeal;
- senior level appointments/personnel changes;
- new projects and funding opportunities;
- endorsements/awards for your work;
- feedback/evaluations of your work – particularly if it is work that they are supporting;
- investments by your group in your own work and personnel.

Newsletters

One way to keep organisations informed about all of the above is to send them your newsletter. If you decide to include organisational donors in your circulation, then this should influence the content and style of your newsletter.

It wouldn't be appropriate, for instance, to bemoan the loss of a particular funder in your newsletter, or to talk about a project going disastrously wrong. Your newsletter will need to be more of a PR vehicle than it might be if it just went to all volunteers and colleagues. *The DIY Guide to Charity Newsletters* (see *Further information*) can give you more guidance.

Some organisations won't want to receive your newsletter – they simply don't want to receive so much paperwork. Rather than ringing or writing round to everyone before sending out your newsletter, you might send a 'sample copy' and ask people to opt out if they don't want to receive another one. You might also give them the option of receiving an update on e-mail or on a website, if you have that facility. This is an environmentally responsible option that groups are increasingly offering.

E-mails

An e-mail version of your newsletter could be text without any pictures. It could be a faithful reproduction of your newsletter that arrives on the recipient's computer desktop which they can read on screen or print out (this costs more to put together than a simple text e-mail).

You can keep in touch with more straightforward e-mails too. E-mail is quick and easy to use, but sometimes people are tempted to dash off a note which they send without checking. Mistakes often creep in, and sometimes it's hard to pick up the tone of the message, so do take care.

Personal contact

Nothing beats personal conversations for building a strong relationship. When time doesn't permit a meeting, then a chat over the phone is helpful. If you can meet face-to-face so much the better.

Again, it's a matter of judgement as to when it's appropriate to call a funder, and what you might ring to discuss. But, if you can work out the right sort of pattern for those funders who appreciate a call, you can make a note on your database about when you last called and when you should make contact in future.

Not only will it help you to remember what you talked about and when is a good time to ring, it will help your colleagues if you aren't around to ask.

Face-to-face meetings are invaluable. They might be arranged when you're going to be 'in the area' where the funder is based. You might invite your donor to see you at your place of work. This enables them to see what else is going on. People are pressed for time, so these meetings need to have a clear purpose. This could be as simple as 'an update on progress', but it needs to be defined and a time limit placed on the meeting.

One small charity providing advice to vulnerable young people has half a dozen regular organisational supporters. The charity's director phones all of them at least once every two months to tell them what has happened recently and what the charity has planned. They also receive the charity's newsletter, which elaborates on some of these issues. And they are sent formal project reports.

The charity sent out a brief questionnaire to the funders asking them if they received enough information, and what format they preferred. They all felt they were sufficiently informed and they welcomed the different methods of communication. All six said that they found the director's phone calls the most useful and informative way of keeping in touch because the calls gave them a 'better feel for what is going on'. They found the project reports informative but 'less enjoyable'.

Networking and meetings

You don't always have to meet your funders on a one-to-one basis. In fact, networking and meetings can be a useful way of meeting new funders as well as existing ones.

Sometimes it can seem to be an effort to get out to these meetings when there's so much to do back at base. And you don't often see immediate results. But they are definitely a good way of mixing with your current funders and keeping up your profile. They provide an opportunity for you to talk to your funders about different projects and initiatives, enabling you to get to know them better. If other potential funders are attending, your current supporters can help introduce you; acting as a good endorsement.

Regular letters to the right people

We use so many different means of communication these days that it's easy to overlook the more traditional methods such as letters. A chatty, informal letter can be highly personalised. It can convey just the right amount of information for the funder concerned.

Newsletters provide a lot of information, but they might be a bit broad for some funders. Phone calls can be very targeted, but you have to think on your feet. Letters allow you to think through exactly what you say. You might want to write some personalised letters to go with your newsletters. You might write when you have something specific to ask or tell your funders.

Annual reports and annual general meetings

A final way of staying in touch with organisations is through annual reports and annual general meetings (AGMs). You can send out your reports and invite funders to your meetings. Equally, you could ask for their reports and attend their meetings.

If you are going to send out your annual report to funders, then you need to consider this when you put it together. Of course, if you are a charity you will have to meet the detailed requirements of charity law. But you can make your report attractive and go into detail about particular projects if you think this will interest funders. You can also look forward, and talk about future plans and funding requirements. See *How to Produce Inspiring Annual Reports* (details in *Further information*) for more ideas.

If funders are coming along to your AGM, then you will need to think about the exact nature of the event. The last thing you want to do is bore your funders. You want to thank them, excite them and inspire them. If there are difficult issues to discuss you can't hide these things, but you can prepare for them. And this preparation might involve briefing your donors about any problems in advance, so that they aren't unexpected.

The advantage of receiving your funders' annual reports is that you will know how they have spent their money over the past year, who else they have supported and how they have justified this. You will get a greater understanding of their motivation, their plans and future funding opportunities. Attending their AGMs is another opportunity for a chat with some of the key personnel.

8

Involving organisations in your work

Many organisations will be happy to stay in touch from a distance. But some will want to see your group in action, and others will want to get quite involved – usually in connection with a specific project they have supported. Most organisations like to be consulted. And they will appreciate a public acknowledgement of the support you have received.

In this chapter we suggest some of the ways you can show your funders different aspects of your work, involve them in decision making and give them credit for their contribution.

We cover:

- Showing your work in action, through different media
- Developing different types of direct face-to-face contact
- How to work with organisations on your advisory board
- Ways of consulting organisations through workshops and surveys
- The importance of publicly acknowledging an organisation's support
- The difference between sponsorship and donations
- The need to remember the individuals who work within organisations

Showing organisations your work

There are two main approaches to demonstrating your work to funders. Indirect contact involves using different media to explain what you do.

In some cases you can send them reports, photos and other materials. You might produce videos or put information on a website. These materials can help to show your work in action, capture the smiles of those involved, and reproduce comments from people who have benefited.

Direct contact, seeing things in the flesh, can be even more affecting. But sometimes it just isn't practical.

We are going to look at some of the options for indirect and direct contact below.

Indirect contact

You can choose from a range of materials to demonstrate your work in action.

Literature

We have already discussed annual reports and newsletters in the previous chapter. They can give a real feel for your projects, as well as conveying straightforward information. There are other publications you can use to show off your work to organisational supporters. These include:

- **Individual project reports** – produced with your donors in mind and giving formal feedback on progress.
- **Documentation compiled by project participants** – project diaries, project photo albums, project graffiti boards and so on. The comments come directly from those involved and funders will receive the unmediated views of people benefiting from their funding.
- **One or more photos and captions** – which funders can use for their own reports or newsletters.
- **Copies of leaflets, posters and other promotional materials** – used to attract people to use your services or to become involved.

Videos

You might also make a video, or assist members/users in making a video. Videos can capture a range of different opinions, give a dynamic presentation of your project, and show how people's lives have been affected by a piece of work. Videos can be fairly expensive and time consuming to produce. However, they can be very powerful at changing someone's mood and mind. With new, cheaper digital cameras, the production costs are coming down. You might even be able to make a video diary an integral part of the project – so that the production costs are fully covered.

A group providing information on health issues to young people received funding for a drama project. Young people from a secondary school and three feeder primary schools devised three short plays to explore issues around mental health and bullying. The funding also included a sum towards a video – of work in progress, the performances and the discussions afterwards.

Copies of the video were sent to all the organisations that had supported the group, and also to schools and other interested bodies in the area.

Websites

Websites can also be used to show your work in action, although they are probably referred to more by individuals for personal reasons than by organisations checking on how their funding has been used.

You can report on work in progress – in words and pictures. Different parts of the site can feature the views of different participants. And you can make websites fairly interactive by inviting comments from people who visit the site. Websites evolve as projects develop, so your funders can see how things change over time.

You won't have to send anything out to your funders except a reminder of the web address. And you should ensure the site is frequently updated.

A group encouraging older people to volunteer in their local community set up a website. The site contained news and information on various projects – including an initiative to link older volunteers with local schools. Some of the schools worked on literacy and IT projects with the older volunteers, and they worked together to develop different parts of the website.

One of the project's funders set up links to its own website, and also became involved in an e-mail storytelling project (where different e-mail recipients added a paragraph to the story before mailing on to the next storyteller).

Direct contact

There are also more direct ways of demonstrating your work to your organisational funders. You could take representatives from your group, or from a particular project, to see your funders. You might make a joint presentation at a conference or similar event. But in the main, you will probably want your funders to come to you.

Events

You can put on special events for one or more funders. If the object is to demonstrate your work in action, then you need to make sure you have something to show them. Putting on a special lunch or dinner might make them feel good about you, but it won't fulfil your purpose of giving them a taste of your work in operation.

So, what sort of event might you hold?

You might organise a special **visit** or trip to one of your projects – where people are shown around, take part in some of the work, and meet those who are directly involved.

You might hold an **open day** where people can just drop in at any time – meeting staff, volunteers and so on. This is more informal than an organised visit. But it needs a little effort to make it sufficiently interesting. Open days might be more appropriate for larger numbers of individual donors than organisational supporters.

You might organise a **training session**, talk, or workshop on your premises. This could be more or less directly related to your work, but it could incorporate a **tour** of particular projects. In a way you are adding value, and making the event sufficiently tempting with the training or talk. Once the funders are a captive audience, you are making the most of the situation by showing off your work.

Exhibitions

As well as running one-off events, you might put on an exhibition over a longer period. This could feature photographs, videos, project reports and other ingredients to bring your work to life. An exhibition can act as an historical record; and you can show off all those things you have achieved and are proud of, as well as those things currently in progress.

An exhibition enables donors to drop in at their own convenience, so you might be able to show your work to more organisations this way. It can also give you and your colleagues a confidence boost, because you can step back and see what you have achieved.

Including organisations in decision making

In this section we run through some of the ways you could involve organisations quite actively in your decision making.

Think tanks, committees and advisory boards

Many groups find it helpful to work with specially-convened advisory boards, committees or 'think tanks'.

Such bodies are usually made up of people with diverse backgrounds and experience, all of direct relevance to the project concerned. They provide guidance, sometimes a direction, and certainly a melting pot for ideas. They most definitely are not focus groups – where you gather a small random sample of people together to survey opinions – or places to 'design by committee'.

Many organisational donors like to be involved in such advisory boards because they have the opportunity to:

- meet other people working in similar fields, and keep up-to-date with other things going on in that area;
- have hands-on influence over the direction of the project they have invested in;
- feel they are making a contribution in skills and experience, as well as in financial terms.

To get the most out of such committees you will need a skilled chairperson/facilitator. The meetings will need to be carefully planned, so that people feel they are making a valuable contribution and giving their time wisely. And there also needs to be sufficient flexibility to spend time discussing a matter that arises in the course of the meeting.

When you involve funders in a think tank, they not only contribute their ideas and keep abreast of developments, they often also get drawn into supporting new projects.

A charity providing respite care to families with disabled children had an advisory board for its holiday projects. The board included five main organisational donors.

An advisory board meeting was called so that the charity could discuss plans for two specially-adapted holiday caravans.

At the end of the meeting people were chatting generally, and someone mentioned their own forthcoming holiday and their experiences of sifting through different brochures. The advisory board then started to discuss the production of a holiday brochure featuring the charity's services, holidays and other holiday facilities for disabled travellers. A company representative on the advisory board believed his organisation would fund the production of the brochure and asked for a proposal...

Workshops

You might not invite all or any funders onto an advisory committee, yet you might want to consult them on certain matters.

One way of doing this is to hold a workshop, or a series of workshops for funders and other interested parties. Such workshops could be very similar to advisory board meetings, but they might be a little more active.

You might use a facilitator to raise a range of issues, and then ask delegates to brainstorm or work in groups to come up with ideas and suggestions.

An animal welfare group ran a series of consultative workshops for organisations that had donated money or services over the previous five years.

Each workshop lasted just an hour – some were held at lunchtime, some over breakfast, and some were 'twilight sessions'.

During each workshop the delegates discussed why they had supported the group in the past, and what they hoped it would achieve in the future. They then moved on to discuss the group's plans to work with homeless young people and their pets. Some funders expressed their reservations at the project: they were particularly concerned about public opinion. They were uncertain about their organisation's position and only felt able to give their personal views. Others were supportive and felt that more could be achieved through the work than had originally been planned.

One funder felt very strongly that the animal welfare group should work in partnership with an advice agency to provide a more integrated service to the homeless young people. The funder introduced the two community groups to one another and they put together a pilot project which was funded by a national grant-making trust.

Surveys

Another way to find out the views of your funders, and involve them in decision making, is through surveys.

You might conduct such surveys over the phone or by post. One method that is increasingly common is the quick fax-back survey. Such surveys usually involve just a single sheet of A4, with some prompts and lots of space for ideas and comments. Offering a fax number for a quick reply usually means a high proportion of the surveys are returned.

If you carry out a survey, don't forget to explain how the information will be used, and why you are gathering people's views. Then, once you have collated your findings, share them with everyone who took part, to show that you are acting on the information.

Also, read through your survey carefully, and test it out on someone independent. They can help you spot ambiguous questions, gaps in the information provided (like your return address or fax number!) and spelling mistakes.

It's always worth allowing people the option to remain anonymous if they wish. You might find that you get some more controversial or honest replies this way.

A charity providing advice and information on drugs and substance misuse sent out a questionnaire to all organisational donors. The survey was asking for their views on plans for a new information booklet. A mix of comments and opinions came back, including one from a funder that had already sponsored a similar pack produced by a local authority education department. The charity followed up this information and obtained a copy of the pack, which it felt it could use, along with an additional sheet giving local contacts.

The education department supplied the charity with 500 copies of the pack at a reduced cost. Even when the charity had also paid for the production of local information sheets, the sum involved was less than it would have invested in the project from its own reserves.

Giving organisations credit

Saying 'thank you' for a donation is important. So too is publicly recognising the support you have received. At the same time you can show you are proud of an organisation's funding. If an organisation feels good about your work as a result, it might want to continue and build on your relationship.

Saying 'thank you'

It seems so obvious to say that you should thank an organisation for its funding. But unfortunately some people forget.

You might also want to say 'thank you' at different times and in different ways.

When you are first offered support, you might want to say 'thank you' over the phone or in writing. Sometimes it can feel more real if you put it in writing: confirming that you heard the offer correctly!

Then when the money arrives – particularly if it is paid directly into your bank account or by cheque – you might want to say thanks again. This will reassure your funder that the money has arrived.

There will be public events and occasions on which it's fitting to say 'thank you' to your donors, so that everyone is aware that this is where your support came from.

And you might want to say thanks again as your project draws to a close. At this stage you are thanking your donors for making the project possible. You are thanking them for all of the things you have been able to achieve, not just for the financial contribution itself. It's this final 'thank you' that could prompt your donors into giving you additional money, when they can see how their money has been well-spent.

Branding

Branding is important to a lot of organisations. They want other people to know that they have given you support. They want more people to know about their organisation and their values.

If an organisation has sponsored a project then you can give as much prominence to its logo and messages as you like, and it wants, in return for its money. If, however, it has made a donation you need to be more sensitive. Sponsorship buys an organisation association with your work. It is paying for the value of this link. And it pays VAT on such a contribution.

A donation is a gift. There isn't supposed to be any service provided in return. So, while you can give written thanks for the support of an organisation and reproduce its logo, it needs to be a bit more subtle.

You might include information about the organisation in your project literature; you might give it a credit on your project letterhead. You would be unlikely to have its banners everywhere and incorporate its name into the title of the project. If you are in doubt, ask the organisation and its lawyers for advice on what's possible. Then think about what is acceptable to you and the project participants.

Lists and plaques

You can say a more lasting kind of 'thank you' for organisations' support. Depending on the type of project, you might produce a list of funders or a plaque to hang on the wall.

This is particularly appropriate if you have received a number of donations for a capital project. Alternatively, if it's more of a revenue-based project you might produce a photograph capturing the essence of the work, with a list of funders. You might then send such a memento to everyone involved, including your donors.

A company made a donation for an environmental project on a housing estate. Local residents cleared the area, cleaned up a pond, planted a meadow and designed some children's play equipment. They also paid for a wooden sign to be carved describing the project. This sign mentioned the company's support.

A photo of children playing, whilst others are maintaining the area beside the sign, hangs in pride of place on the boardroom wall of the company.

Public relations

You can thank your organisational donors publicly through any media coverage you receive.

If you are sending out a news release then you can include details of your funders. Your news release announcing the donation will obviously include information about who has made the gift. But you need to refer to your donor in other releases too. A simple sentence at the end of your news release will usually be ignored, so you need to integrate this information into the release itself. You might include a quote from your funder. You might refer to your funder in a quote from your own spokesperson. Or perhaps a representative from your donor organisation will be featured in a photograph, but not handing over a cheque if you can avoid it. So many charities send newspapers this sort of picture that it is less likely to be used than a more unusual image.

If you manage to get a radio or television interview then you should try to mention your funder, but this should sound natural and not like a bolted-on advertisement.

Don't forget to keep copies of any press cuttings or interviews so that you can send these to your donors for their own records.

Acting as a 'case study'

Another way of saying 'thank you' is by being willing to act as a case study for your funders. Just as you want them to recommend you to others, they often want to present groups like yours as examples of the good work they support. In a way they are asking you to be a reference for them.

They might ask you to write a short article, provide pictures, or a comment for an annual report, newsletter or something similar. You can show your gratitude by being ready and able to help, and by meeting their deadlines.

Don't forget the individuals

Finally, don't forget that you are thanking organisations, but you are also thanking individuals. It's the individuals within organisations who make the case to their colleagues about the need for your work and the reasons why they should support you. It's the individuals within organisations who come up with good ideas to help you develop your work. And it's the individuals who can provide moral support when problems arise. Thank them personally.

Individuals act for organisations, but they also make decisions about their personal giving. And that's what we're going to look at in the next section of this book.

Benefiting again from individuals

Individuals have various complicated reasons for giving to charity. And if you can understand why, and show your appreciation, you might secure additional – even ongoing – support. In this chapter we look at the different types of individual giving and some of the ways to encourage additional donations.

We cover:

- The different patterns of giving and the various motivations individuals have for donating to a good cause
- How to encourage regular giving
- How to plan your mailings to reflect a person's history of giving

From small beginnings

Just as we saw that many organisations want to start with a small, low-risk donation, many individuals begin in a similar way. Almost unthinking, they might pop some money into a collection tin, buy a ticket for an event or take part in a raffle. You might never see them again. It's only when you manage to get their details, so that you can stay in touch, that you're likely to be able to build a relationship with them that brings you repeat donations, moving on to more regular support and, possibly, a legacy when they die (see the diagram below):

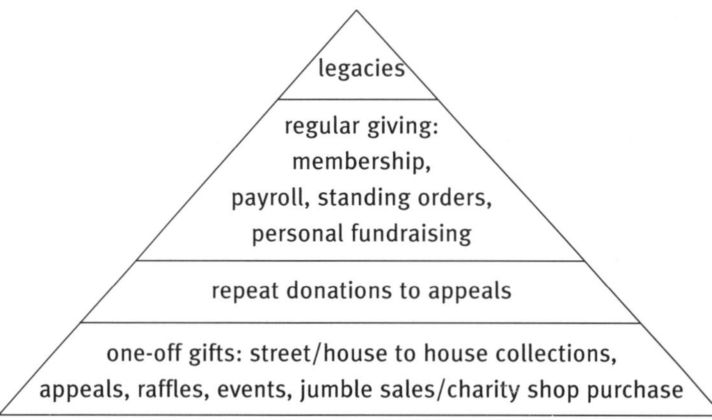

People, like organisations, are free to move between the different layers in the pyramid. They are also constrained by their personal financial circumstances. But it is possible to secure their commitment, to nurture them, and benefit from small and regular donations.

One-off 'random' gifts

When people make small one-off gifts to your organisation this can be valuable, but hard to track and hard to build on. We have described one-off gifts as being quite 'random'. It just so happens that there is a street collection as the person is walking by. They might think briefly about the cause, but they are unlikely to consider the matter in great depth. That's why many organisations provide stickers, mementoes or badges to remind the donor of the cause they have just given to.

Research by Professor Adrian Sargeant found that one in ten lapsed supporters had no memory of ever giving to that charity in the first place. He says, 'Lapsed donors have significantly poorer views of delivered quality [of service] than active supporters and in particular tend not to regard the organisation as providing adequate feedback about how their donation has been used.' ('Improving donor retention: how can charities build loyalty?' in *Dimensions 2000, Volume 2*; see *Further information*.)

Sadly for the collector, though, they don't have a record of who has made the donation. This is at least possible with a door-to-door collection, though you don't necessarily know how much each person has given.

People attend events because they are attracted by what's going on, more than by the cause they happen to be supporting. Similarly, they enter a raffle in the hope of winning the prize, and in passing make a donation to a good cause.

So, the important thing is to build on every opportunity to give information about your organisation and work, whilst trying to record people's names and addresses for your database (with their permission, of course).

The one sure-fire way of getting such information is by running an appeal through an advert or by mailing people (from a purchased list). Most people who respond will provide their contact details, and you will have information to work with. The first thing to do will be to send them a note of thanks and possibly an information leaflet. You can write again at a later stage with further requests for donations.

Repeat donations

Once you have captured information on your database about individuals, you can check whether or not they give to your organisation for a second and third time. Who's to know how many repeat donations you are receiving from those loyal people who always buy goods at your jumble sale, or who regularly pop some money into the static collection tin at the pub? If they are anonymous you can't build a relationship with them.

As soon as people respond more than once to your appeal you can start to get an idea about what motivates them to give. Patterns might start to emerge. And you can tell them about the benefits of tax-effective regular support.

Ongoing regular support

In the main people will not weigh in with ongoing regular support if they haven't first got to know your organisation, and begun with a small donation. It's not unheard of, though. And particularly with payroll giving, if someone is offered a choice of five different possible organisations to support they might commit despite making no previous donations.

Ongoing regular support might take the form of a membership subscription. This would be renewed each year and members might get voting rights, or particular information. In the past some people have given through covenants to make their gifts tax efficient, although recent legislation has made this unnecessary. And others, as we have said, might give through a payroll giving scheme such as Give As You Earn.

Another way in which some individuals give ongoing regular support is by fundraising on behalf of an organisation. This might be through personal sponsorship activities. Anything they do in this way has to be with your agreement, they can't just fundraise on your behalf without asking. If someone starts fundraising in your name without your permission, then you can take legal action to stop them.

Your regular supporters can also help you by spreading the word – acting as ambassadors on your behalf. This is the ultimate in 'pyramid selling' or 'pyramid fundraising'. You can provide them with appeal literature and ask them to distribute it to friends and family with a personal recommendation. All donations are sent directly back to you, and you have control over the contents of the literature. It comes with a personal endorsement, though, that can make all the difference. And you can then capture data on all the people who are motivated to give. At this stage you can start to build your own relationship with them.

A charity providing advice and support to refugees and asylum seekers had a group of regular individual donors who were actively involved in projects as well as providing financial help. The charity realised that recruiting new donors was proving quite difficult, because of people's personal prejudices, a local public campaign against its work and some misleading press articles.

To redress the balance, charity workers met with the editor of one newspaper and explained their work in great detail. The paper printed an article and invited a debate on the letters page which still contained some negative views, but a great deal of information was provided. At the same time, the charity asked its core of regular supporters to invite their friends and family to a challenging public meeting. These regular supporters followed up the meeting by talking to their friends and relatives, and distributing project leaflets and the charity's annual report.

The campaign led to an increase in the number of donations by individuals by approximately 70%. And it helped to double income from individuals in that year.

Legacies

Not all regular supporters will move on to make a gift to your organisation in their wills. And not all of those leaving legacies to your organisation will have made donations in the past.

However, there is often a connection between past giving habits and bequests or legacies.

Someone might leave you a specific sum of money or item/property. However, they might leave you the amount of money which is left over after all the other legacies have been distributed. Or they might leave you some property which reverts to your organisation when the relative living in it dies.

As you can see, legacies are complicated and you need to take proper legal advice on any work you undertake in this area. *Legacy Fundraising* (see *Further information*) can give you more help.

It's certainly hard to evaluate the success of any promotional work you do around legacies, as the results of such work might come through many years in the future.

The important thing is to approach this subject with sensitivity. Have information available, and perhaps choose to approach certain donors personally or in a very targeted way.

You might run a campaign to encourage people to make a will, and then almost as a rider suggest that people make a donation to your organisation.

You might be more direct and ask people to add your organisation to their wills. Alternatively you might approach funeral directors and tell them about your organisation should any families want to offer 'memorial giving' in place of flowers.

Clever mailings

There are many different ways, then, in which individuals might choose to make donations to your organisation. They will have their own motivations and history of gifts to your cause. If you make a note of this on your fundraising database then you will be able to do 'clever mailings' to reflect this.

For instance, if someone has recently decided to contribute through payroll giving, you wouldn't want to include them in a mailing highlighting the virtues of Give As You Earn. You might, however, want to send them a thank-you note and encourage them to spread the word to their friends.

If someone has recently made their first ever response to an appeal, then you wouldn't want to overwhelm them with a request to make a will in which they remember your organisation. You might, though, send them a very big thank you and a 'welcome' introductory information pack explaining some of the many different things you do.

Perhaps some donors have 'signed up' to give a sum of money over time. You will need to make contact with them just before this commitment ends to see if they would like to do something similar in the future.

If some people have given generously in the past, but have now stopped giving, you might want to send them some up-to-date information. At the same time you could invite a small donation to get them back into the giving habit. Or you might invite them to an event so that you can demonstrate your work in action.

Whatever combination of mailings you do, you will need a plan for the year to ensure you don't contact people too often and don't miss any out.

With your plan for the year you will be able to take decisions on whether some mailings can be combined to save on postage (for instance by sending a leaflet with a newsletter). You might also realise that the numbers for a particular mailing would be so small that it would be more cost effective to ring the people up, or visit them for personal contact.

Your mailings might contain different appeals or fundraising devices but all will probably be personalised: addressed to the individually named donor. You will also need to make it easy for the person to respond, perhaps by enclosing a reply-paid envelope, or by giving an easy-to-complete form and freepost address.

The design of the leaflets themselves will vary depending on the particular appeal, but will always reflect your organisation's branding so that your donors immediately know that the appeal comes from you (an organisation they trust and have some degree of history with).

You will have some ideas about what motivates your donors to give. Pictures are helpful because they catch the attention and can convey a great deal. Sometimes emotive language can be off-putting, whereas an image can be genuinely moving.

Your words need to get to the point of the appeal quickly, and make things tangible for your donors. What could their £5 achieve? How much could be done with £25? Short, punchy sentences are essential. And make sure you actually ask for a contribution.

You will want to keep every individual donor on your database informed of what is going on. But, just as you will send different appeal letters to different types of donors, you might keep in touch in slightly different ways, depending on their track record. In the next chapter we discuss some of the options.

Example of a mailing plan

Donor type	Jan	Feb	Mar	Apr	May	Jun	Jul	Aug	Sep	Oct	Nov	Dec
1st time*	project appeal					newsletter			annual report	xmas catalogue		newsletter xmas card
Repeat			project appeal			newsletter tax effective giving letter			annual report	xmas catalogue		newsletter xmas card
Regular**			project appeal			newsletter wills letter			annual report	xmas catalogue		newsletter xmas card

Notes

** 1st time donors to be sent a thank-you letter and welcome pack as gifts are received.*

*** Regular donors to be sent a reminder note one month before their commitment ceases.*

All to be sent an emergency appeal letter if required.

10

Keeping individuals informed

You are probably not uppermost in your supporters' minds most of the time. How can you get them to think about you, care about you and make additional donations? We look at some of the ways you might stay in touch.

In this chapter we consider:

- The need to stay in the minds of your supporters
- What aspects of your work and achievements will be of interest to individual donors
- Different ways to stay in touch with individuals

Staying in touch

People are bombarded by different images, appeals, sales pitches and information. Hundreds of companies, charities and others are all vying for their attention. In such a competitive environment you are easily overlooked, if not forgotten. So, it is important to make regular contact with individual donors: to remind them of your existence, to tell them about what you have achieved, to inform them of your plans, and to ask them for their continued support.

According to Adrian Sargeant this is vital if you want to hold on to your donors – 'To engender loyalty, charities need to improve both the quality of their communications and the choice that they offer in respect of communication.' ('Improving donor retention: how can charities build loyalty?' in *Dimensions 2000, Volume 2*; see *Further information*.)

What are they interested in?

You will need to think carefully about what will interest your diverse mix of individual donors. Will someone who made a donation to your building appeal be interested in how successful you have been in raising money to run a training programme with your volunteers? They might be, but you wouldn't ring them up or send them a note especially to tell them about this. You might, however, include a small article in your newsletter to let people know about this, along with other news.

People will usually be interested in anything with which they have had direct involvement – by giving money, attending an event or adding their signature to a campaign. If they have made a contribution of this kind, you would be justified in writing to them or ringing them up with information.

As it's hard to predict what will interest particular people, sometimes it's good to offer them the chance to opt in to receiving certain bits of information.

An environmental group with a large membership brings out a quarterly members' magazine. This provides news and information on a broad spread of its work. In addition, it produces monthly updates on school-industry links, volunteer action, and public campaigns. Some members like to receive all of these additional updates. Most have opted for one of the three, because that is their particular area of interest.

Newsletters

Newsletters are a good way of sending out information on the many different things you're involved in. Even if a topic isn't of particular interest to the reader there are ways that you can make the article lively and readable.

A good headline, followed by a punchy summary of the article below, can tempt people in. The article should be written in a similar way to a news release, with the first sentence summing up the essence of what follows. Short sentences and short words will help. And the style of writing should be relaxed and chatty.

The articles should be full of quotes from different people to bring it alive. And good, clear, action-packed photographs can transform a newsletter.

Individual donors might welcome the opportunity to send letters to a newsletter, so that it becomes more interactive.

And you can also use your newsletter to highlight gifts that you have received – saying 'thank you' of course. At the same time you can explain some of the tax-effective ways of giving on a regular basis, or include an article on the importance of making a will. This can be quite a gentle way of introducing these topics to some of your less frequent donors. If you focus on personal stories then you will also interest people who are already signed up to giving through a covenant, or who have already included a legacy in their will.

Letters

Letters are a more personal way of staying in touch with individual donors. There are various occasions on which personalised letters will be appropriate. In some cases a mail-merged letter is all that is needed, so that it contains the correct salutation and address. In other cases you will want to write an individual letter which is created for that one donor (or their family).

Letters might be appropriate in the following circumstances:

- as cover notes to go with appeal leaflets, newsletters or other mailings;
- to say 'thank you' for a particularly generous gift, or for an individual's fundraising efforts;
- to thank a family if their relative has left a legacy or bequest in their will, or if they asked for donations instead of flowers at a funeral;
- to make an unusual request of some of your larger donors;
- to remind regular givers or members that their covenant or similar commitment is coming to an end and will need to be renewed.

Phone calls

Sometimes you will want to speak to your individual donors by phone. You might want to ring them up if they have made a very large donation. If they have been giving regularly and could take advantage of a more tax-effective method you might simply send them a leaflet. However, you might want to ring them first to thank them for their loyalty, and suggest they think about a different approach.

You might want to contact your top 20 individual donors always by phone when you are asking for a donation. You will soon get to know whether or not they prefer this approach, and whether it yields more money for your organisation.

E-mail

E-mail can be a good way to keep in touch with donors. Not all individuals have access to e-mail, but it is growing in its use.

You might make newsletters and updates available by e-mail. Or you might encourage a more active dialogue with supporters, encouraging them to send questions by e-mail, or setting up a noticeboard for them to post comments for other supporters to respond to.

A community group established by parents of children with a rare genetic illness set up a website and encouraged parents to contribute to an e-mail noticeboard. The families shared information and experiences, and contributions came from people around the world. The noticeboard contained the usual rules about not posting commercial or offensive material. Occasionally the group added news of its latest projects or research updates to the noticeboard.

The group carried out a survey of parents who paid a membership fee, and 90% of those with access to the Internet said they used the e-mail noticeboard at least once a week and felt it was a highly useful service. Every time the families used the site, they saw the group's name and logo. Not surprisingly, they felt highly involved in the work of the organisation and well-informed.

Project literature

There are, of course, more traditional ways of keeping people informed about the work of your organisation. You can produce leaflets, project reports and other literature.

The key thing is not just to send it out to everyone on your database. Sometimes it will be appropriate to send individual donors a project report if they have contributed directly to that piece of work. At other times you might want to list some of your literature in a newsletter, or publications catalogue, and invite your donors to request anything they are interested in.

Occasionally you might want to send out a leaflet about your work along with one of your appeal letters.

Annual reports and annual general meetings

Once a year you can invite your individual donors to your AGM. A small proportion will usually turn up. But you can certainly send everyone your annual report.

You might want to send a covering letter with the annual report highlighting particular sections that you think will be of interest to different donors. This doesn't have to be personalised to every individual, but it could be tailored to the broad categories of donor, or to people who supported different appeals.

11

Involving individuals in your work

Some people are happy to send a cheque through the post, or to give a donation in the street without seeing your work in action or being involved in any other way. Others welcome the chance to see how their money is being put to good use. They might also want to be consulted and to have some sort of influence over the direction of your organisation's work. And whatever their level of involvement, it is essential to find ways of thanking donors appropriately.

In this chapter we cover:

- Using different media to demonstrate your work in action
- How to use direct contact with your donors to good effect
- Different ways of staying in touch with individuals
- How to consult your members through surveys
- The role of members within a community group
- How to consult individuals through representative bodies
- The need to say 'thank you' to individual donors
- Different ways in which you can acknowledge the contribution of individuals

Showing individuals your work

You can explain your work in a variety of ways.

Materials

You don't have to demonstrate the details of your operation in person. There is a range of materials you might use to bring your work to life, for those who can't spare the time to come to you.

Literature

We have already talked about how you might use projects and annual reports to keep people informed. This sort of literature can also be used to show your work in action.

The literature you send to individuals will be probably be written in a different way to the materials you send to organisational donors. You might use less jargon, go into less detail on the mechanics of the project, and give less of an evaluation of progress.

A charity working with young people at risk of offending ran a summer project. As part of the work the young people put together a four-page magazine. Copies of the magazine were sent to all the charity's individual donors, with a note explaining what was achieved as a result of the project.

You don't have to produce huge publications, and sometimes the simple things have more impact. A dramatic picture produced as a postcard can be mailed to certain individual supporters, with a note about what's going on.

Websites

You might also put reports and pictures on a website so that people can take a look at their leisure. Individuals are more likely to use this way of staying in touch than your organisational donors. If you hope to keep people informed in this way you will need to update the site regularly (otherwise they'll look once or twice and stop going there). And you will need to remind people to take a look – promoting the address on all of your literature.

A young people's advice project set up a website for a number of reasons, including the need to keep their individual donors informed of progress. When they did some research into how well the site was used they found that people visited it once or twice, and then didn't return. They asked why this was the case, and the response was that the site hadn't really changed much, so what was the point? As a result the project set up a training scheme with a group of young people who put together a new website and carried out regular updates. They discovered that the 'news' section of the site was visited more often than any other area. And when they produced an advert asking for donations, they placed it within this section.

Direct contact

So far we have talked about ways of showing individuals your work in a fairly indirect way. You can also show your work to them more directly.

Open days

Open days are a good way of demonstrating your work in action. Open days for organisational donors might be for a few people at a time. Those for individual donors are likely to be designed for larger audiences.

You might simply throw open the doors on a normal working day, and invite everyone on your database to pop in. This might not be enough to tempt people along. One thing you might do is to incorporate some activities or taster sessions to attract people. You might hold a fundraising event at your premises, so that people have fun and see what you do at the same time.

It's always useful to know how many people you are expecting, so you might want to send out invitations and ask people to ring or write for free tickets.

A charity providing training and work placements for people with learning difficulties wanted to show individual donors its work in action. The previous year it had advertised an open day to people who had supported its work. However, only a handful had come along, and they had stood around for a few minutes, chatted to the director of the charity, had a coffee and departed.

This time the charity decided to do something different. So, it invited its individual donors to a lunchtime presentation by its celebrity patron. Over 100 people attended. After the lunch they saw the training in action, and they were each given a gift made by the charity's trainees.

After the event each of the attendees was sent a letter thanking them for coming, and asking them if they would contribute towards the cost of some new training equipment. Over 70 people responded, and the charity hit its target.

Visits

As well as inviting people to your main base, you might organise visits or tours to see projects in action. As with open days it will be important to know how many people might want to come along, and to ensure the event is sufficiently interesting to attract people.

A community arts organisation works with deafblind children, visiting special schools and play schemes. Each year it develops a new performance designed to involve the children in various ways. The group runs 10 development and rehearsal sessions, before embarking on its full programme. The performers invite up to 10 individual donors to attend each of these rehearsals, which are provided free of charge to the host schools and play schemes. This has proved to be a successful way of motivating the donors to give again, and at a higher level.

Personal involvement

Your individual donors don't just have to be spectators when they see your work in action. They can get involved themselves.

If your work has some practical elements to it you might want to invite your donors along to help out. They might clear pathways, help in play schemes, become mentors for young people, or drivers for outings. You are not necessarily asking them to become a regular volunteer. The point is that if they roll up their sleeves and have a go, they will have a far greater understanding of what your operation is all about. They will hopefully have a positive experience. And they will have something physical to remember, which all helps you to stick more firmly in their minds.

An organisation working with older people has several reminiscence projects running in different day centres. The group invited some of its regular, individual donors to become involved in a weekend of events to record and document people's stories – on audio tape, on camcorder and in writing.

During the event the group talked to the donors about different forms of tax-effective giving. Afterwards several donors decided to give donations through their payroll, and they talked to colleagues about their experience – inspiring others to get involved too.

Including individuals in decision making

Just as some individual donors want to see your work in action, many will want to be consulted. There are various ways of encouraging them to have their say.

Surveys

One way to find out the views of your individual donors is to carry out a survey. You need to be absolutely clear about the point of the survey: is it to find out more about your donors themselves, or is it genuinely to consult them? Many people quite rightly get irritated when they receive a questionnaire which claims to be seeking their views, and which then asks them in great detail about their job, marital status, income level and spending habits.

If you are conducting a survey to build up your donor profiles, then say so and give donors the option not to have their information passed on to a third party. Tell people that you want to send them the right information, and ask for their support for appropriate projects so that you don't waste their time. However, if your questionnaire is genuinely seeking their views you can make the replies anonymous. This will guarantee you can't add further details to your database (and you won't be selling the information on to someone else).

So, when might you want to seek your donors' opinions? In terms of timing, probably no more than once a year if you want to get the maximum number of replies. There are various occasions on which it might be appropriate to seek their views. These include:

- **Times of change** – when you want their views on a possible change to your organisation's structure, or focus of work.
- **Reviews** – when you want to find out what they think of your work, or your relationship with them, so that you can make improvements.
- **Ideas** – when you are looking for their creative suggestions about future projects or areas of work.
- **Needs and wants** – when you want to establish their needs or desires for information, involvement, events and so on.

An equal opportunities group carried out a survey of its individual donors, asking them about 'significant gaps or opportunities' that they could identify for the organisation. Many of the responses made minor suggestions about additional information that could be included in newsletters, and ways of raising the group's profile in the area. One respondent felt that the group could be offering its training to local businesses, as well as to people within the public and voluntary sector. He also offered to get things moving through his involvement with the local chamber of commerce. The group felt that this was a positive way of raising awareness, and ensuring equal opportunities good practice was spread more widely. It also took action on some of the smaller suggestions!

Members

You might want to offer individual supporters the opportunity to become 'members' of your organisation, if this is appropriate. Members might be given certain voting or decision-making rights, or they might be consulted at certain points throughout the year.

If individual donors become members then not only do they feel more involved in the running of the organisation, they also make a regular commitment to give money or a subscription.

Representative bodies

Another way of involving individual donors in decision making is through representative bodies, or advisory groups. Sometimes these committees have a mix of organisations and individuals. In some cases it will be appropriate to set up different bodies for different types of donors.

Whatever the constitution of the committee, it will be important to ensure that any individuals are representative of the wider mix of individual donors. For instance, you might ask for nominations and invite people to vote for representatives.

These committees can be helpful in taking decisions on particular projects and areas of work. You might also want to consult them when you are planning some fundraising literature or activities.

A small organisation for disabled people has an advisory group of individual donors. Whenever a new fundraising leaflet is being drafted it is sent to members of the committee for comments. The advisory group has helped to plan a fundraising event that members felt would appeal to other donors. And the group also came up with an idea for a new project to set up an informal support group for carers.

As you can see, individual donors can contribute ideas, time and moral support as well as their money. So, don't forget to say 'thank you' and let them know how grateful you are.

Giving individuals credit

Many people give for private reasons and are quite shy about their gifts. But some are proud of their donation and welcome public attention. It's important to find out which camp your donor falls into before putting their name in lights. But if they are keen to be acknowledged there are various ways of doing so.

Saying 'thank you'

Even if someone wants to be discreet about their giving, you should still thank them for it. You will want to thank them when you receive their first donation, or when they sign up to give on a regular basis. If they are giving by standing order or through payroll giving, then you might want to send them a note each year to say 'thanks'. In this note you can show them the total of their donations for the year, and say how this money has been used.

This will reassure them that their money is being used appropriately. And it will show that you aren't taking their donations for granted. It might even prompt them to give again, or increase the amount they are donating.

Plaques and rolls of honour

Plaques are fairly often used to recognise a contribution from an organisation. They can also be appropriate in the case of individual donors. If someone leaves a substantial sum in their will, then you might want to honour this with a plaque in a relevant place. Sometimes smaller gifts can be acknowledged in a similar way. For instance, donations that pay for seats or benches often have small plaques with the name of the donor.

One shopmobility scheme received several large gifts from individual donors to pay for motorised scooters, to be used by disabled and older shoppers. Because every major donor had given enough money to buy a scooter, the charity attached a small plaque to each one with the names of the donors.

If a large number of people have contributed to the overall sum raised a plaque might not be appropriate, or feasible. However, a roll of honour might be possible. This is a long list of all donors, usually in alphabetical order, which is printed and put on display. You don't usually state the sum of money given by each person.

The same roll of honour might be published in different booklets.

An educational charity has produced rolls of honour to list the names of all of its donors contributing to every major project. These have been printed alongside pictures of the project in action, and they hang around the walls of the charity's office.

The rolls of honour have been reproduced in its annual report. And copies have been sent to donors too.

Certificates

Certificates, like the rolls of honour described above, can be sent out to donors in recognition of their gift. They need to say more than 'a big thank you to Karen for her gift of £10 to the building appeal'. It might not even be appropriate to list the sum of money given, as this can seem embarrassingly small when it's put onto an official document like this.

It might be better to produce a well-designed certificate which contains some information about how the donation will be used.

Certificates might be more appropriate for donations from children and young people, particularly if they have paid a membership subscription.

A community arts centre receives donations from a range of sources. Membership makes a valuable contribution. As well as receiving regular subscriptions from adults – who can join at different levels – the arts centre has a children's club. All of the children receive a certificate, explaining that they are members of the arts centre and that their money has helped to pay for performances by theatre groups, dancers, puppeteers, musicians and magicians. The certificate features a stunning montage of photos from these performances. And many children hang their certificates on the wall.

The arts centre is regularly contacted by parents of other children who have seen the certificates, asking if they can have a certificate too, and asking how much it costs to become a member!

High profile

Another way to show your appreciation for your individual donors' contributions is by making sure the project has a high profile.

If you manage to get a lot of publicity for your work, and make sure you stress your appreciation of all the support you have received, this can be very rewarding for your donors. Donors won't be named personally, but the reference to their kind support will still be meaningful.

And maintaining a high profile will help you to attract new supporters in the future.

12

Evaluation

Some of the techniques we have outlined throughout this guide will take quite some time to produce repeat donations. And some are quite indirectly linked to the act of giving itself. It will be hard to assess how much a donor has been influenced by, for instance, reading your annual report. However, some things can be measured and evaluated and we discuss these in this chapter.

This final chapter covers:

- The importance of monitoring and evaluating your donor development work
- How to monitor your progress
- Different evaluation techniques which you can use to assess donor development

Assessing your success

It is important to reflect on how effective your donor relations work has been. It takes up time, and it costs money. So you need to be sure that the investment produces the intended results: commitment, repeat donations, new ideas and other outcomes.

You will need to return to your original plan to remind yourself of your aims and objectives, and your goals. These should guide any assessment of your success. And don't forget the importance of some of the things you hoped to achieve apart from the financial improvements. You might be a lot richer in terms of ideas, new projects and volunteers, but might not have triggered a big increase in donations. You might feel that all of these gains justify your programme of donor care.

Monitoring

Monitoring is essential if you are to assess what you have achieved. It's up to you to decide what to monitor. But the key is to make sure it's an ongoing process. If you leave everything until you write a report at the end of the year you will have lost some vital information.

You can monitor things like:

- how many times you have been in touch with different donors;
- how many responses you have received to a particular mailing or appeal;
- how much money you have made from each mailing or appeal;
- how much money has been donated, on average, per contribution;
- how many people are giving through regular tax-effective means, and how much this has grown over the year;
- how many organisations have made contributions in kind, and how many have gone on to make larger donations;
- how many people have requested information on making a will;
- how many people have turned up to events and open days.

As you can see from the above list, which certainly isn't exhaustive, there's an awful lot of data you could gather. You need to decide what will be relevant and informative. And you need to set mechanisms in place to gather this information.

A lot of the data might be stored in your computer, and built up over the year. But it's worth pulling the statistics together at regular intervals so that you aren't overwhelmed by the task when you are carrying out your review. You might also find some useful data that makes you change direction halfway through the year. For instance, if you find that hardly anyone has been requesting your detailed project updates, then you might not need to produce them in future. Or, if you are inundated with requests for your leaflet on how to make a will, you might want to offer telephone advice or home visits to your donors.

But what do you do with all of this information? You need to attach some values to it. Do you think that an increase in membership of 10% is good, indifferent, or simply to be expected? You might want to discuss the figures with colleagues so that they can help to interpret them.

A 'friends' organisation which fundraises for a local school looked at its donations over a two-year period. It found that:

- after mailing out its half-yearly newsletter, it received unsolicited repeat donations from two per cent of people and organisations on its database;
- no-one had requested its leaflet on making a will, which had been promoted in a low key way (mentioned on other leaflets, and in some newsletters);
- its appeal letters proved more successful when they followed an event, such as the Christmas Fayre or Summer Fete.

As a result of this analysis, the organisation took the following action:

- future newsletters contained prominent details of how to make a donation in a tax-effective way (the following year repeat donations went up to four per cent);
- a special flier was sent out, promoting the will leaflet (five per cent of people on the database requested a copy);
- major appeal letters were sent after the two main events of the year (and secured substantial donations);
- additional smaller events were introduced in the spring and autumn, before smaller appeals were made.

Evaluation

So far we have talked about gathering quantities of information through monitoring. But it's also vital to form some views about quality and how things will have an impact on different areas in the future.

Review with colleagues

You might have a review meeting with colleagues to kick off this process. Find out their reactions to various mailings and campaigns, and ask them if they think things could be done differently or improved in any way. Have they heard any comments? Is there any anecdotal evidence on the impact of your work? Have you received particular letters or feedback?

Meet with donor representatives

If you have advisory boards or think tanks, with representatives from your donors, then you might want to talk to them about how they feel about your support and contact. Invite them to be frank about what they like and what they think could be improved.

Survey donors

You might survey a sample of your donors to find out what they think about particular initiatives or leaflets. You don't need to send questionnaires to all of them, just a sample. You might conduct your survey over the phone, by fax or by post. Again, invite ideas and encourage them to be open.

Make value judgements

In the end you will need to make some value judgements. You will have to decide on whether you think holding an open day for donors has helped them to get to know you better, and given you more of a feel for your supporters, as well as encouraging more committed giving.

Benchmarking

After you have conducted your first evaluation you will have some figures to work from in future. You might not know whether a 10% membership increase is good at this stage. But next year when it rises by another 15%, you can make some comparisons and set further targets.

It helps to give you evidence on which to plan for the future.

Looking ahead

Looking after your donors can seem like a never-ending task.

Some donors only ever make one contribution, others stop giving, or leave you a large legacy when they die. There's always a need to build up support from new individuals and organisations. And all of these donors need to be thanked, kept informed and encouraged to give more again in the future.

It's hard work, but you'll be rewarded when your donors tell other people about your work, give you hundreds of good ideas, volunteer some of their time, and when they give you some more money to support your work.

Further information and advice

In this section we outline details of some of the helpful organisations, publications and sources of advice mentioned throughout this guide.

Organisations

Association of Charitable Foundations (ACF)
2 Plough Yard
Shoreditch High Street
London EC2A 3LP
Tel 020 7422 8600
Fax 020 7422 8606
The UK-wide body representing trusts and foundations. ACF runs seminars and conferences for its members, helps to develop good practice guides, and encourages the exchange of information and advice between hundreds of trusts and foundations.

Charities Aid Foundation (CAF)
Kings Hill
West Malling
Kent ME19 4TA
Tel 01732 520000
www.cafonline.org (for news and case studies)
www.ngobooks.org.uk (to order books)
The Charities Aid Foundation provides financial services to charities and donors, including the Give As You Earn payroll giving scheme. Books previously published by CAF are now available through the Directory of Social Change.

Charity Commission
Harmsworth House
13–15 Bouverie Street
London EC4Y 8DP
Tel 0870 333 0123
The Charity Commission regulates charities in England and Wales, and maintains a register of charities. The Commission publishes a range of helpful guidelines on matters such as SORP.

Corporate Responsibility Group
Business in the Community
44 Baker Street
London W1M 1DH
Tel 020 7224 1600
The Corporate Responsibility Group of Business in the Community represents some of the biggest charitable-givers in the business world. Some of these companies make their donations through associated grant-making trusts.

Data Protection Registrar
Wycliffe House
Water Lane
Wilmslow SK9 5AF
Tel 01625 545745
The Data Protection Registrar can provide more information on the need to register under the Data Protection Act.

Direct Marketing Association
Haymarket House
1 Oxendon Street
London SW1Y 4EE
Tel 020 7321 2525
This organisation provides advice and information on direct marketing.

The Directory of Social Change (DSC)
24 Stephenson Way
London NW1 2DP
Liverpool office:
Federation House
Hope Street
Liverpool L1 9BW
Publications and subscriptions:
Tel 020 7209 5151
Fax 020 7209 5049
Marketing and research:
(London) Tel 020 7209 4422
(Liverpool) Tel 0151 708 0136
Courses and conferences:
(London) Tel 020 7209 4949
(Liverpool) 0151 708 0117
Charityfair:
Tel 020 7209 4949
or 020 7209 1015 (exhibitors)
DSC is a registered charity set up to help voluntary organisations become more effective. It provides information and training and organises Charityfair, the biggest annual forum for the sector.

Federation of Charity Advice Services (FCAS)
11 Upper York Street
Wakefield WF1 3LQ
Tel 01924 239063
This organisation represents charity information bureaux, charity advice services and others supporting voluntary groups in search of funding.

Institute of Charity Fundraising Managers (ICFM)
1 Nine Elms Lane
London SW8 5NQ
Tel 020 7627 3436
Fax 020 7627 3508
ICFM produces good practice guides, and represents fundraisers for the voluntary sector. It runs training sessions on a wide variety of fundraising matters, and holds an annual conference.

National Association of Councils for Voluntary Service (NACVS)
3rd Floor
Arundel Court
177 Arundel Street
Sheffield S1 2NU
Tel 0114 278 6636
NACVS is the national body for councils of voluntary service. It produces a directory of these local development organisations.

Publications

All titles in this list published by the Charities Aid Foundation (CAF) or the Directory of Social Change (DSC) are available from DSC Books, 24 Stephenson Way, London NW1 2DP. Call 020 7209 5151 for a free publications list. Prices were correct at the time of going to press but may be subject to change.

Benn's Media
Volume 1 – UK, Volume 2 – Europe and Volume 3 – World
2000. £152 (1 vol), £300 (2 vols) or £325 (3 vols)
Miller Freeman
Riverbank House
Angel Lane
Tonbridge TN9 1SE
Tel 01732 362666
This directory contains contact details for local and national press, radio and television, with useful contacts in specialist publications.

Building a Fundraising Database Using your PC
A step by step guide for small voluntary organisations
Peter Flory, CAF, 1999. £11.95

Data Protection for Voluntary Organisations
Paul Ticher, DSC, 2000. £12.95

Dimensions 2000
CAF, 15th edition, 2000. £10 (Vol 1), £12 (Vol 2), £25 (Vol 3), £32.50 (set of 3)
Volume 1 – Income from government sources
Volume 2 – CAF's top 500 fundraising charities
Volume 3 – Patterns of independent grantmaking in the UK
Volume 2 includes the 1997–98 league tables on the voluntary income of CAF's top fundraising charities and a review of the long-term income trends of the top 400. Volume 3 presents the results of the first survey of independent trust and foundation funding distribution in the UK.

The Directory of Grant Making Trusts 1999–2000 (DGMT)
16th edition, CAF, 1999. £89.95 (3 vols)
Volume 1 contains indexes by geographical area, field of interest, type of beneficiary and type of grant. Volume 2 is the main register, listing trusts in alphabetical order. Volume 3 gives detailed commentaries on 250 major trusts.

The DIY Guide to Charity Newsletters
Chris Wells, DSC, 1996. £10.95

The DIY Guide to Public Relations
Moi Ali, DSC, 1999. £12.50

Effective Media Relations
A guide for small voluntary organisations
Ian Gilchrist, CAF, 1997. £7.95

Find the Funds
A new approach to fundraising research
Christopher Carnie, DSC, 2000. £12.95

Grantseeker CD-ROM 2000
Release 3, Feb. 2000. £58.69
An interactive CD-ROM version of the DGMT. From 2001 Grantseeker *will be amalgamated with DSC's* CD-ROM Trusts Guide *to produce one comprehensive database for researchers.*

A Guide to the Local Trusts
Sarah Harland, Louise Walker, DSC, 2nd edition, 1999. £17.95 each
These guides provide specific information on trusts which focus their grantmaking on particular geographical areas: Greater London, the Midlands, the North and the South.

A Guide to the Major Trusts
Volume 1 – the top 300 trusts
Luke Fitzherbert, Dominic Addison and Faisel Rahman, DSC, 7th edition, 1999. £19.95
Volume 2 – the next 700 trusts
Dave Casson and Sarah Harland, DSC, 4th edition, 2000. £19.95
Volume 3 – a further 400 UK-wide trusts, with further details on major trusts in Northern Ireland, Scotland and Wales
Sarah Harland and Louise Walker, DSC, 1st edition, 2000. £17.95
These guides give a critical analysis of the grantmaking of the UK's top trusts

and foundations. The **CD-ROM Trusts Guide** *contains all the information from Volumes 1 and 2 of* A Guide to the Major Trusts, *plus all four local trust guides. The CD-ROM will merge with the* Grantseeker CD-ROM *from CAF from 2001.*

How to Produce Inspiring Annual Reports
A guide for voluntary, arts and campaigning organisations
Ken Burnett and Karin Weatherup, DSC, 2000. £12.50

Improving donor retention: how can charities build loyalty?
Adrian Sargeant in *Dimensions 2000*, Volume 2 (see above)

Legacy Fundraising
edited by Sebastian Wilberforce, CAF/ICFM, 1998. £14.95

Third Sector
Lime Wharf
Vyner Street
London E2 9DJ
Tel 020 8709 9050
This magazine provides news and features on developments in the charity world.